Living High in the Dirty Business of Dreams

LIVING HIGH IN THE DIRTY BUSINESS OF DREAMS

HAMISH TRUMBLE

First published 2025

Copyright © Hamish Trumble 2025

The moral rights of the author have been asserted.

All rights are reserved, except as permitted under the Australian Copyright Act 1968 (for example, fair dealing for the purposes of study, research, criticism or review). No part of this book may be reproduced, stored in a retrieval system, communicated or transmitted in any form or by any means without prior written permission from the author.

Cover design by Tony Leishman

Typesetting by BookPOD

ISBN: 978-1-7635823-2-3 (paperback)

 A catalogue record for this book is available from the National Library of Australia

To Billy Zane

"The Phantom moves like a shadow in a dream, and strikes like lightning." Old jungle saying.

CONTENTS

Last Night I Dreamed of Matsuko Deluxe	7
Last Night I Dreamed of the Trams of Nagasaki	11
Last Night I Dreamed of Wolverine	15
Last Night I Dreamed of Immanuel Kant	17
White Van Fever	19
Last Night I Dreamed of Brute Bernard	23
Last Night I Dreamed of Jeff Kennett	25
My Father's Swing	27
Last Night I Dreamed of Brown Rice Pesto	31
My Beard Joyeuse	35
Last Night I Dreamed a Dream of Japan	37
Last Night I Dreamed of Graham Greene	41
My Coffin	57
Death in Venice	63
The Queen	67
My Shop	73
The Song of the Lobster	75
Macro the Wonderdog	77
A Dog in the Manger	79
Macro The Wonderdog's Dream	83
The Marriage of Finn Mac Cool: or I Saw A Half Eaten Orange Tree, And It Was My Mother	87
Port Melbourne	89
Traffic Light	91
Latin Rap (Catullus LI & LXXXV)	93
The Ballad of a Good Looking Man	99
The Proper Jesus, 11/12/09	103
Ironing the Hankies	105
Plantation	109

Nouvelle Caledonie Nocturne	111
The Love Song of Cagliostro and Macro the Wonderdog	115
From My Desk in Head Office of the Defence Department	117
Dog in Art Manifesto, Promulgated at the Dog in Art Exhibition, Collingwood 1986CE	119
The Barassicon	121
The Extraction	123
Bad Hamish	127
Lawn	133
Random Thoughts as I Swim Laps	135
Mayakovsky - A Centennial*	141
On Attending the Funeral of a Casual Acquaintance	145
Far North	149
San Remo Mio Amore	153
Naming Byron Bay	155
I'm Special	159
A Poem to Celebrate Helen's 50th Year as My Mother	161
Untitled	165
Podiatry	167
A New Idea	169
Scraping the Bottom of the Barrel	173
A Demon Rave – Queen's Birthday Clash, 2015	175
Fantasia for Leaf Blower	177
The Song of the Big Fat Babyboomer	181
Belmont Market Observations	185
The Spiders - Bristol Road, Torquay	187
Last Night I Dreamed of the Giraffe	191

BESTIARY

Dromedary	197
Canary	198
Popinjay	199
Shag	200
Spider	201
Goose	202
Sloth	203
Dog	204
Baboon	205
Yeast	206
Swine	207
Penguin	208
Hare	209
Mole	210
Ant	211
Walrus	212
Eel	213
Grizzly Bear	214
Oyster	215
Sphinx	216
Viper	217
Queen Bee	218
Louse	219
Rat	220
Ibis	221
Worm	222
Dragon	223
Raven	224
Koala	225
Dodo	226

Toad	227
Goat	228
Fox	229
Shark	230
Lobster	231
Rooster	232
Possum	233
Thylacine	234
The Blowfly in Winter	236
Acknowledgments	237

SELECTED WORKS

Allow me to introduce myself. Call me Hamish. Some of you may know me as The Magnificent Hamish, others as Z.Z. Byron, one quarter of the seminal performance poetry troupe Byron Dangerously which blazed meteorically across Melbourne's comedy cabaret scene in the 1980s, still others as mrbooksywooksy, toiler in the second hand book mines, a bottom feeder in the grand ecology of books. It is my life's work, far from cathedrals of literature like Readings or The Book Grocer, to trawl through the great mass of books on its inexorable way to landfill to rescue anything curious or rare fit for resale. It is in this capacity that I long ago observed that there are far too many novels being published, especially literary novels, way too many. Was it not the smartypants Frenchie Raymond Queneau, himself a novelist whom we all should read, who pointed out that all novels, indeed all works of fiction, descend either from the Iliad or from the Odyssey, providing with this self-evident truth the last nail in the lid of the coffin of the novel? And yet novelists keep churning them out, so many that paleontologists of the future will notice a curious strata of fossilised paperbacks encircling the Earth and defining our epoch. Long ago I proposed a moratorium on all novel writing, especially literary fiction, to commence immediately. I call it the MiLAN KunDERa memorial moratorium. Let us instead increase production of fine non-fiction - letters and postcards, social and art history, biographies of nice interesting people, amusing anecdotes, gossip and travel writing, and poetry, especially performance poetry - the form at which I excel. Yes, poetry is my metier and this book my masterpiece.

These works are a selection of materials I have wrought over the past 45 years, some written on scraps of invoices cadged from my in-tray at various public service offices, some committed to memory for performance, some contained in envelopes returned to me by publishers unwilling to bite. They represent a lifetime of toil in the salt mines of literature, a lifetime that started out with so much promise. My childhood was spent with my nose in books and no television or social media to distract me. I was an indiscriminate reader, consuming whatever I could lay my mitts on - from Biggles to War and Peace, from Dune to LOTR, from Swallows and Amazons to Quo Vadis. From Molesworth to Hunter S. Thompson. From The Magic Pudding to Notre Dame de Paris. And then, after HSC I was accepted into Jesus College Cambridge to study English Literature. I remember I was sent a reading list that represented the bedrock of the English Literature Canon, to be under my belt before I commenced. All of Jane Austen, all of George Eliot, most of Dickens, most of Shakespeare, etc, etc. I duly read everything I had not already read.

My proud parents sent me off, never expecting me to return, and confident, I think, that I would in time produce the great Australian novel.

Last year I attended the 50 year anniversary of the Class of '74 at Jesus and caught up with some old friends and colleagues. One old boy sat next to me at lunch and told me that as we walked together to sit our very last exam I told him that I hated poetry. I was quite adamant, he said. He said he has been dining out on that anecdote for 50 years. I said, it sounds like me, but of course, it isn't true at all. I think I must have had in mind the kind of poetry the Cambridge English Department pushed then that I hated. After all, what was I talking about? Piers Plowman, the Pearl, all of Chaucer, The Faerie Queen, Paradise Lost, The Rape of the Lock, The Prelude, Keats's Endymion, Shelley, Don

Juan, The Idylls of the King and the works of Matthew Arnold, and all this to a boy who had already read and admired Walt Whitman, Allen Ginsberg, Edith Sitwell and Don Marquis wotthehell. Of course I hated Poetry. At that time I thought much more of the novel, and I read the lot, from Tristram Shandy and Tom Jones to Thackeray to Flaubert, Melville, Joyce, Woolf, Saki, Wodehouse, Chandler, Vonnegut and Dick.

I was fortunate to have one teacher who was interested in the nouveau roman, deconstruction, post-modernism, post-structuralism, Barthes, Foucault and Derrida. He and I played cricket in the Jesus Third XI and we held our tutorials under the ancient thatch of the delightful Jesus pavilion during our batting innings while I got my head around the new order. By the end of my stay at Cambridge I was supersaturated with its gruelling syllabus. I remember not cramming for my final exams by reading William Burroughs Jnr and Ian Fleming's 007 novels while I drifted along the Cam in a punt sipping Pimm's No 1 Cup. So Poetry was my least favourite subject, until I had the bright idea of writing my own. After that, it wasn't long before I realised that no-one wanted to pay me to publish it, so I should read it out loud with plenty of expression to drunken patrons of pubs in Fitzroy. If it didn't pay, it was fun for all that.

So, bear in mind that these works were intended to be heard, seen in performance, experienced viscerally and when you read them, see if you can't conjure up in your mind a tall, devilish handsome fellow belting them out in a smokey, crowded bar while you rub shoulders with his wildly appreciative fan base. You may even heckle - I can deal with that.

LAST NIGHT I DREAMED OF MATSUKO DELUXE

I dreamed I was playing Pachinko
On the Evangelion machine
And next to me on the One Piece machine
Was Matsuko Deluxe, celebrity drag artiste,
And the sound of a trillion steel ball-bearings
Cascading incomprehensibly
Was like diamonds crushed in a black hole
Was like all the Kamahl records on Earth
Burning in a Nuclear Holocaust
Was like the first second of the Big Bang
And I was winning
More and more
Impossibly more
So much more I almost awoke
But then Matsuko Deluxe spoke
"Tell me, oh sweet Lady Hambone,
What brings you to Japan
Land of the Immaculate Bullet Train?"
"It is you, Oh Matsuko Deluxe, plus-sized diva,
Hard hitting and controversial
For you are my inspiration, my Muse,

My spirit guide in the delightful miasma
Of Japanese TV
And now that I have earned great honour
And fame
On the senior Sumo circuit
I intend to forge a career like unto yours."
"But how may I ask, oh plucky one,"
Said Matsuko Deluxe in my dream
"Do you see yourself achieving
This admirable yet unlikely goal
As a straight cross-dressing foreign devil,
A slovenly uncouth barbarian
With unpleasant personal habits?
For you are not a gay man, is it not so?"
"But wise and insightful Matsuko Deluxe"
I replied," Was Dame Edna gay?
Or even a man? (Some thought not)
Was Danny La Rue? Or Dick Emery?
Or Matt Lucas or David Walliams?
Or Liberace even??
But were they not beautiful?
And flamboyant?
And worthy of adoration, as you are?
I may not enjoy *'L'amour de l'impossible'*
As we used to call it at Melbourne Grammar,
And I do not have your gravelly voice
And sharp tongue
But I have your physique and hysterical fits
And, what is more, enormous height
I have stage presence
I have the voice projection
I have great expression -

"More expression!" cried my gleeful children
At bedtime storytime - and
The camera adores me.
Proto-entrepeneur Helena Rubinstein
Decreed that Beauty is Power
And I am that Beauty, that Power"
In my dream Matsuko Deluxe, Power Gay,
Conceded that I have a dream
"Fierce Lady Hambone, you have a dream
I see that clearly now
But have you considered a sponsor
To lubricate your passage
With fat wads of cash
And other untaxable benefits?"
"Oh sagacious Matsuko Deluxe
Street wise and hip,
You have penetrated to the nub
But my people are in negotiations
With the people of
The Japanese Pork Industry Peak Authority
And my pitch to them
Is my slogan
Lady Hambone's motto
"Eat More Pork!!!!"
And that, dearly beloved, woke me up

LAST NIGHT I DREAMED OF THE TRAMS OF NAGASAKI

Rattling, clanking and squealing through
Fairy rings of Brutalist concrete mushrooms
And garish neon Christmas lights
That radiate around ground zero
As you Americans would call it
I smell again the sand brake ozone
And the screaming flanges in my dream
Recall my mother's mnemonic aide-memoire
"69 best on the line
4D not for me"
As she sent me off to school
Clutching my Gladstone bag
Ever ready to raise my cap
To passing adults
And give up my seat for anybody
More venerable than me
Or risk a scathing letter
Read out at assembly
"Some Boy
Has impugned the honour of Our School
Our Anglican Faith in Jesus the Jew
Our great British Commonwealth
Our beloved Melbourne Football Club...."

A severe warning never forgotten
Not to take the wrong track home
But to brave the hooligan boys from De La Salle
With their arcane lacrosse racquets
And run the gauntlet of Lauriston girls
Even more terrifying in their snide mockery
But there were pleasures too
Frenchie the Conductor
Swinging like a monkey from the hand rails
And the sweet intense sensual smell
Of the Nigger Boy Liquorice Factory
In Hawthorn Road
In my dream I sit in Leaving Physics
Contemplating the question
What makes the tram go round the corner?
Brainbox P...... M...... raises his hand
Inertia he opines
Wrong! and I have a go
The flanges on the wheels
Correct!!! Such a surge of pride!!
I still remember even in dreams
However,
I have since learnt from Richard P. Feynman
Joint Nobel Laureate in Physics of 1965
That we both were wrong,
All three if we include Tony Smith
Our physics master with the legs of a dancer
The wheels of the fixed axle bogies
The parts that sit on the track
Are not cylindrical as you might imagine
But conical sections tapering outwardly
And so as centrifugal force asserts itself

This ingenious feat of engineering
Enables the inner and outer wheels
To turn at different rates in cornering
No, that's not quite right
They travel different distances in rotation
And smoothly negotiate the curve of track
Without the need for a differential
And by constant minute correction
Keep the train in equilibrium
On the long straight sections that take me
Off to the Land of Nod

LAST NIGHT I DREAMED OF WOLVERINE

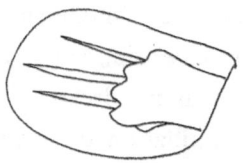

I really dreamt of Hugh Jackman
But I couldn't think of his name
And in my dream I confounded him
With Tom Waits
Latter day beatnik
Because I had seen a picture of him
On Facebook as you do
Being goosed by Bette Midler
In my dream
So I racked my brain to remember
Their wretched names
In my dream
I was trawling through an unfamiliar city
Trying to get to an open air performance
It was Grease
And Hugh Jackman was starring
In my dream
Someone had given us tickets
But when we got there I couldn't find them
Hugh Jackman saw I was struggling
He came over and asked our names
I said I had tickets somewhere
He said not to worry and gave us tickets

In my dream
Then he went out on stage to open the show
But no, he announced with a flourish
That Hamish and Maxine had arrived
And I was at once ashamed and exhilarated
In my dream
Humiliation and pride
Anxiety and ego
Woke me up sweating
Maxine said later that my dream
Was inspired by the man in the ceramics shop
In Ochi, Japan
Who, when he learnt that we were Australian
Said "Ah, Greg Norman,
So sad Olivia Newton John"
And mimed tears of grief down his cheeks
Which would explain Grease
But I reckon my dream
Has to do with my show biz aspirations
After all
Hugh Jackman oozes musical theatre
Does he not?
But has he done comedy cabaret?
Like me
Has he done performance poetry?
Like me
Nor am I aware that he has done drag
Like me.
So there you have it Wolverine
Retract your vibranium fingernails
Or else Lady Hambone
Will scratch your own eyes out

LAST NIGHT I DREAMED
OF IMMANUEL KANT

I dreamt I was playing Pokemon
In the Pokemon Club in Imari
With several monsters out of Dragonball Z -
Frieza, Broly and Android 17 -
They had come down from their forest lair
And we were playing for money
With coins made of porcelain
And I was winning
More and more
Impossibly more
So much more I almost awoke
But suddenly
I recalled the first book I sold.
It was Kant's Critique of Pure Reason
I found it in the Op-Shop
I thought I ought to read it.
I did try but life is so short
So I put it in the shop window
As a whimsicality.
A flippancy in a frock shop.
And lo! It sold.
The boy who bought it

Had been sniffing around M... S......
- I forget his name -
but he must have liked the cold
For he had signed up for a season
In Antarctica to warm up.
He was looking for something meaty to read
On the lonesome ice station.
He told me his research project
Was going to be on comparative rates
Of fingernail growth
Under extreme climactic conditions.
Good for him.
And good for Kant
Even though he never his whole lifelong
Ventured more than nine miles from Konigsberg
Like a dog on a tucker box,
Let alone to Antarctica
The pristine Pokemon region of my dreams

WHITE VAN FEVER

Preamble

Since the dawn of civilization
And the invention of personal property
A secret guild has controlled its traffic
On donkeys, camels, bullocks,
Wagons, handcarts, sleds, barrows,
In barges, ships, and ferries,
Porters, Sherpas, bearers.
How else did Catullus shift his bed to
Late republic Rome?
Or Shakespeare get his new sets for The Globe?
Or Victor Hugo lay his new carpet in his
Second empire Paris apartment?
Or Sir Edmund Hilary and Tenzing Norgay
bogart their oxygen tanks atop Mt Everest?
And here at last we stand, our backs up against
The tsunami of climate change
The crisis of peak oil
In Melbourne, rocky outcrop in an ocean of stuff,
With only the van between us and cataclysmic annihilation

It is the Fellowship of the White Van I sing
I, the little known seventh son of Tracy,
Hamish Tracy, pilot of Thunderbird Seven,

the white ThunderVan that shuttles
Stuff from Brains to Lady Penelope.
Our lovely French Vanilla vans are
White corpuscles of the urban circulatory system
Trucks and trams are its free radicals
Buses are its plaque
We are Tribe HiAce of the Long Wheel Base
And we don't give way
We are Kevin Murray in a hurry
Get out of my way and stay on the left,
Napoleon
Euclid will need to amend his Fourth
Postulate to cope with the hook turn
at the corner of Exhibition and Bourke
Out of my way,
There's an emergency chop chop delivery to Cheltenham
Hard rubbish in Rowville
Goon-drinking trouble-making teens needing ichpig in Ipswich
Op shops to trawl in Traralgon
Garage sales in Grantville
Deceased estates in Deacon
A show-n-shine in Shepparton
A farm clearing sale in Sale
A Dead Letter Office auction in Officer
A police profits of crime auction
in Reservoir
A swap meet in Swan Reach
No crow flew -
No bee made a line -
Nor did Patrick Dangerfield part his hair -
Straighter than the white van on a mission
Supercar tyres for Phillip Island

Artisan beer for Alberton
Air needs conditioning in Canterbury
Interiors need decorating in Deakin
Some poor bastard is locked out of their house
Their car
Their smart phone
Data needs protecting in Portsea
Gates and Garage Doors need automating
Cheesecake for Chelsea Heights
Classy carpet needs laying in Laverton
Brakes and Clutches for Club Terrace
An asset needs managing in Mornington
Mexican Cantina needs taco shells in Sherbrooke
A consignment of black belts for the Dojo in Docklands
A dog needs washing in Williamstown
Video conferencing needs some support in Sunbury
A pool needs chlorine in Clunes
Sensitive files need shredding in Loch
Graffiti in Greensborough needs a solution
An espresso machine in Moe needs service and repair
A carpet needs cleaning in Carlton
A pest needs controlling in Collingwood
Concrete needs sawing in Sassafras
A corporation needs catering in Kew
Italian sausage needs refrigeration in Reefton
The surf is sick at Woolamai
Pelmets flyscreens truffles pie,
Removals, drainage, storage, logistics,
Designer kitchens, architectural joinery,
Cabinets - commercial and domestic
The man with a van is your man
Or woman

It is easier for a rich camel to back through the
eye of a needle into the kingdom of heaven than
to park a van upstairs at the Victoria Hotel
And yet it can, it must, it will be done
Before all else
And that, O well-beloved, is why they call it
a van

LAST NIGHT I DREAMED
OF BRUTE BERNARD

In the frozen wastes of Canada
Felling the Douglas Fir with his bare hands
Eating bales of hay soaked in whisky
Driving his whiskers in with a hammer
To bite them off inside
Grunting like a rutting bull elk
His shaggy pelt dishevelled
His horny hide carbuncled
shambling around the ring
Pounding his hideous bear-like thorax
And reaching out his ham fist paw
To tag his femboy lover
Skull Murphy from County Cork
While we three screaming nancies
Wrestling fan brothers
Free at last from hair shirt church
Cavorting like baboons on my Grandmother's
best front parlour furniture
Waited for the Sunday roast
And pavlova
While the grown-ups

Drank beer and sherry in the kitchen.
Did they know?
Did they care?
What ghastly and pernicious troll
They had unleashed in the shabby gentility
Of that quiet middle class enclave?

LAST NIGHT I DREAMED OF JEFF KENNETT

In my dream I was a child
Holidaying at Metung
In the family lakeside love bungalow
Trying to sleep in my bunk
While the grown ups drank whisky
And smoked cigarillos in the kitchen
Next door.
Dad salvaged them bunks
From some decommissioned Navy hulk
While he was building his shack
They were narrow with horsehair mattresses
And they were not comfy
And there was no glass in the windows
Just fly wire, so sleep was impossible
Until the grown ups passed out.
In my dream Dad was hosting
A rowdy Liberal Party pre-selection conference
And here comes Robert Doyle
Disgraced former Lord Mayor of Melbourne

Looking for Dad's shoe polish
And here comes Jeff Kennett
Former Premier of Victoria
Obsessively raking up fallen leaves
And here comes John Howard
Former Prime Minister of Australia
With a glass of red wine in one hand
And picking out an atonal melody
On my piano to put me to sleep.
As if.
That piano Mum gave to a cousin
While I stepped out of the country
For a few years
Because it was our grandmother's
And Mum never expected me to come home
But the cousin went and sold it.
Issues, issues galore
I remember something there
That glided past me followed close by heavy breathin'
I'm not concerned, it will not harm me
Even in my dreams.
But really my dream
Was not about the Liberal Party
Or the family holiday house at Metung
Or my piano
But about Dad
And his stern affability
And his endearing fetishes
And his organisational skill set
And his natural affinity
With Arnold Schoenberg on the goanna

MY FATHER'S SWING

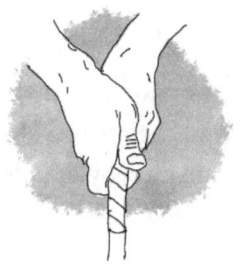

First a little wiggle
And a waggle
A tippy tap
And a snippy snap and then...

My Father's swing was like a gentle tornado
A corduroy swagger
A crisp burnt chop from a bush campfire
A pensive Galilean pendulum
A polite compliment to faithful servants
A judicious nod of respect to Physics
A kiss of persimmon and gutta-percha
A snickety snack of the sound of one hand-
the gloved lead hand at the top of the grip-
Clapping
A saucy wink at the Lizard King
A dream of wild geese in the winter
A black bull's roar in the top paddock
A deferential bow to the Bench
A prelude to a snifter
A rebuff to the vulgar
A good humoured savagery

A sad cloud over the pathetic fallacy
A flip into overdrive
A well bred seduction
A tranquil twist over the yardstick
A memory of the other half
A post-dated cheque to a sly creditor
A smooth transition by double de-clutch
A run over moguls by stem christies
With a timely bend of the knees
A cube of blue before the mangle
A refutation of tripe
A passably bel esprit tram conductor's satchel
The laughter of the jackass
A twinkle in an acuminous lover's eye

His swing was not brutal, like Joe Stalin's
Or unreliable, like Jack Kerouac's
Or mean, like Evelyn Waugh's
Or flamboyant, like Oscar's
Or persnickety, like Henry James'
Or parsimonious, like Charles Bukowski's
Or crabbed, like John Betjeman's
Or bovine, like Ernest Hemingway's
Or vituperative, like Dorothy Parker's
Or flashy, like Kinky Friedman's
Or fussy, like P.G. Wodehouse's
Or belligerent, like Dostoevsky's
Or nervous, like Philip K. Dick's

Not too straight
Not too long
Not too hooked or sliced
Not too showy

The nub of my father's swing was a very
hard thing to put your finger on,
like a shy stool before breakfast

The head of Dad's jigger described a non-
Euclidean arc of rare and unco beauty
Of righteousness in a schism
Of a pearl in flight from swine
Of mist rising from the stomach to the spleen
Of a paucity of ego.
Its purpose was not to hold up play.
Its purpose was the betterment of Man.
And the Ladies.

When I asked him to teach me his style,
he answered gravely, quoting Anatoly Karpov
"But my boy, I have no style"

LAST NIGHT I DREAMED OF BROWN RICE PESTO

Oh Rhumbarallas
Our neighbours
On the sunny side
(Next door neighbours
At one time)
Puissant food art nexus
Caffeine hit in the Fringe plexus

Oh Rhumbarallas
I remember planning
A fine production -
The Revenger's Tragedy -
With David Branson
Over your coffee.
I would play Vindice.
Well, that will never happen now

Oh Rhumbarallas
I remember beating
A leather-clad Chris Barnett
At speed chess in your window
And I never gave him a rematch
Was that rude?

Yes? No?
I think so too

Oh Rhumbarallas
I remember sitting up the back
With Big Shane Marshall
And John Ashton
(The Bard of Fitzroy)
Discussing a band that would become
The Right-Thinking Wranglers

Oh Rhumbarallas
I played for you
My last game of footy -
Artists v Dealers -
(Some feeling there
It nearly killed me)
I took a screamer
On the half back flank
Right in front of Boom Boom
And Pussy.
Second best on ground
I won a bottle of Champagne
(The umpires love a ruckman).
That ground in Royal Park
Since dug up
Replanted with bush, so
No-one will know
The glorious deeds of our youth
That took place there

But get this, Rhumbarallas

It was right there in the new Native Gardens
Of Royal Park
Ghost scene of football long forgotten
That number one son got married!

Glorious indeed
And so it is with you
Rhumbarallas
A ruby reverberation,
A lingering languid mouthfeel
A ghostly echo
Of a whisper in the afterglow
Of Brunswick Street
In the psychogeography
Of Narrm

MY BEARD JOYEUSE

I shall grow a fine new beard
For my Art
And it will be a manly, father of sons beard
Wise like Socrates' beard
Compassionate like Jesus' girlie beard
Inscrutable like Fu Manchu's beard
Tough-as-nails like the Frozen Logger's beard
Soft and wispy like a Bloomsbury acolyte's beard
My beard will be all things to all men
and my ladies will lazily run their fingers through its dainty curls
My beard will tell a thousand tales like Victor Hugo's beard
My beard will glow in the dark like Madame Curie's beard
The force will be with my beard, Obi Wan Kanobi
Steely grey like Odin's beard
Curiously melodious like Demis Roussos's beard
My beard will unite the people like Garibaldi's beard
My beard will realise Plato's transcendent Beard Form,
Of which other men's beards are mere insubstantial shadows
I shall call my beard Joyeuse after Charlemagne's glorious beard
My beard will be stoic like Seneca's beard
My beard will irritate my wife like Hereward the Wake's beard
My beard will be pompous like Louis Pasteur's beard

My beard will be cruel like Barry Manilow's beard
My beard will be rugged and outdoorsy like Natty Bumpo's beard
My strange and loathsome chin will disappear beneath Joyeuse
My lips so thin and bloodless will luxuriate
Beneath my rollicking and obstreperous moustaches
My sallow sunken cheeks will disappear beneath Joyeuse
Oh Joyeuse!!!
Chuck Norris will quail
ZZ Top will quail
Walt Whitman will give up poetry slams
Karl Marx will expostulate
Charles Darwin will ponder
Rasputin will quail
Alan Ginsberg will go to California
Ernest Hemingway will thump his chest
Khal Drogo will quail before thee,
My wonderful beard Joyeuse

LAST NIGHT I DREAMED A DREAM OF JAPAN

Oh House Japan
Land of the Enormous Turnip
Your walls are paper
Like obscure poems
Flimsy and diaphanous
Your floors are socks with a place for the big pinkie
Your ceilings teem with invisible ninjas
Scuttling about politely like Tombei the Mist
Your poets are drunk like ours,
But poised between self abnegation, hilarity
and rigidly elegant protocols
Your little schoolgirls wear Sex Pistols t-shirts
And your gangsters wear Mickey Mouse
Pretty maidens clean your lavatories
And origami the ends of toilet paper rolls
Into chrysanthemums and peonies
Grown men wipe their dogs' bottoms
Trees and streams and fire and dead leaves
Cars and bees and stones and the wind
Space trains and Time itself
All things living and not are sentient.
Admire the diamond spider

Like one of Liberace's rings
Go on, you paid for it
Be careful to dispose of fingernail clippings
Correctly lest the witches find them
Run, run like the clappers
Through the railway station
To get out of earshot of Fur Elise
On the upright piano.
How gracious, how polite
Are your police, saluting me
And bowing as I cross the road
Obedient to the ruling walk sign.
In Hosen-in Temple pilgrims sip tea
Beneath ceiling boards stained
With the blood of 400 slaughtered warriors
A consolation for their restless souls
In Japan you may find a bar
Catering to every vice
From French maids to rockabilly outlaws
Your windows admit light in waves
Or particles, I can't decide which.
Waves I think, like sound or good taste,
And I am suspended in the constructive interference that occurs
When the positive displacements from
the equilibrium of gravity and time meet and coincide,
Oscillating like a tremulous lotus
Like a boogie board between sets
Like a full moon reflected in a maiden's tears
Like a seaweed rice cracker caught between two crows
Like a grey heron on Bald Mountain
And where the rice paddies meet the forest
Where the sea shore meets the wide Pacific

Where the mountain peak meets the sky
That's where the Ghosts and Monsters,
Dragons and dinosaurs
Enter the Peacock Realm
As I did in my dream
Through the fog and rain that periodically stops
And the Earth quakes when the Big Dog walks around
At Kurisumasu with Colonel Santa San
And the bus driver,
Tibetan throat singing
All the way to Fuji San

LAST NIGHT I DREAMED OF GRAHAM GREENE

PART 1

"Many are called but few get up"
Oliver Herford

In my dream
I was sitting at a cafe table
(It was Rhumbarallas I'm sure)
Waiting for an appointment with someone.
I decided to place my diary,
My cheque book, my pencil case
And my pager what I won
As carry over champion
On Sale of the Century
Hosted by Glen "Heartbreak" Ridge
All in a neat pile at my feet
Rather than clutter up the little round table.
As I bent down in my dream
I dropped a small round object
(A coin, a wedding ring,
A Demon's footy badge of Garry Baker?)

Which fell to the ground and spun
Gyroscopically
On the polished floorboards.
When I sat up
Graham Greene was just sitting down
Opposite me.
He handed me a folded paper
Which someone had shown him -
It was a poem I had written -
And he said, in my dream,
"This is the most considerable piece of
writing I have ever read in my life."
These were his very words.
I can still remember them.
I was thrilled and spluttered an incoherent remark.
Graham Greene then proceeded to name
all the authors he admired
(By surname, like small boys at a grammar school)
And after each name he gave a brief phrase
Which explained why their work was
less considerable than mine.
Names and phrases like Waugh, too mean,
Joyce, too inscrutable,
Mailer, too butch,
Borges, too spooky
Hugo, too much detail,
Baudelaire, not enough detail,
Names, names more and more names
Melville, Vidal, Updike, Nabokov, Sterne, Musil,
A roll call, an upper-middle brow honour board,
Haussmann, Colette, Huxley, Powell, Hamsun,
Big names reeling off, Dostoevsky, Chandler, Poe,

Simenon, Dick, Camus, Saki, Grass, Shelley,
Mann, Hesse, Wodehouse, Fenimore Cooper,
Oh! On and on it went
And my ecstasy grew more and more exquisite
As the names tumbled out
Like the one armed bandit's jackpot.
And gradually names even I did not recognize,
Well-read as I am,
And oh my pride and pleasure,
And names more famous for other attributes
Kinky Friedman, Disraeli, Evel Knevel, Dave Warner,
Iceberg Slim,
And still other names I did not recognize at all
Pebblethwaite, Trimble, Elephantini, Tank,
Sidebottom,
And I shuddered with a frisson of angst
And then names I did recognize
But not as authors,
Rimsky-Korsakov, Jagger, Barassi, Curie,
McEnroe, Presley, Dali, Ponting, Feynman,
Gorbachov,
Each name accompanied by its backhanded epithet -
None of which I can now remember -
And slowly I realized that Graham Greene
Was turning into Kevin Rudd,
No, wait a bit, Stephen Fry,
And I saw he was crying,
Like a big fat baby
And I almost woke up.

I call this class of dream
The Dream of Impossible Abundance.
I have it quite often
Usually I find a coin
And another and another,
Soon a few together
More and more
Impossibly more
A pile, a heap,
A chest full to overflowing with bullion
Or a treasure trove
Until the pleasure of random bounty
Is tainted by the dawning realisation
Of its absurdity
Of its impossibility,
And I awake ruefully.
This time I remember thinking
As the dream began to spin
And wobble out of control
Like that tiny round thing
On the floor beneath the table
"Goodness me, if Graham Greene
Likes this poem so much

How much more would he like
'My Thylacine - a dramatic monologue'!"
I got up inspired to get cracking
On the work immediately.
Today is three or four days later.
I am going to do it.
Yes.
Oh my wordy word, yes.

2007.

PART 2: SOUTH GIPPSLAND GOTHIC
OR THE THYLACINE

I wrote that passage in 2007. I can date it by the reference to Kevin Rudd who had just then swung into my field of view. Kevin 07. Today is Friday 29 November 2013. I have just now found the passage in a notebook while I was scrounging up some exercise books for Number One Son who needs them for school. I like it. The passage, not school. It does form a nice introduction for the Thylacine story which began even earlier during one of the El Nino summers of the drought, about 2005. It goes like this:

Call me Hamish.

Some years ago—never mind how long precisely—having little or no money in my purse, and nothing particular to interest me in Kongwak, I thought I would drive about a little and see the South Gippsland part of the world. It is a way I have of driving off the spleen.

In the morning, the morning of the Thylacine, Hamish (that's me) lay in his bed slowly becoming aware of things like a big fat Ernest Hemingway. Out of the hazy fug of a near hangover from precision red wine drinking the night before, he watched particles of dust suspended in the rays of a feeble rising sun lazily milling about like the hoi polloi. Up on the ceiling, daddy longlegs patiently stalked their unimaginable prey amongst their shabby webs. A little higher up, under the roof, scuttling rats anticipated Armageddon, when they would inherit my house. Hamish could hear the crows and the clatter of their claws on his corrugated iron while the fruit ripened on the old pear tree. Hamish's attention floated above his house in what some were to describe later as a golden cloud, others as a blinding flash of pure consciousness, while still others claimed they saw a strange doughnut-shaped flying vehicle. The ghost of Hamish's dog, Macro the Wonderdog, pricked up her ears and sniffed the hay fevered air. Then she went back to sleep. But up and up, on and on went Hamish's attention, through the clear air, cold like charity, through those nimbo-cumulus clouds full of errant hang-gliders and hailstones, through the ozone layer smelling of trams and the seaside, and through the outer atmosphere where the detritus of the space industry - nuts and spanners, old antennas and busted tiles - flew earthwards and burned up with a crackling fizz, and past the cosmonauts frantically working to patch up their rickety space station as it tumbled towards a fiery conflagration in the deserts of Western Australia. Hamish thought briefly of the inexorable approach of the millennium - it was a momentary lapse in his grasp on the time line. The bickering cosmonauts dragged his attention back to low Earth orbit. "You know, Sergei", said Yuri petulantly as he swept aside the tumbling chessmen to recover his space wrench, " I do not agree with your proposition of 0200 hours that all men are either

Platonists or Aristotelians. I believe that Glasnost has made you Eurocentric." Tempers were frayed, and Hamish's attention now shifted into a heightened hyper-sensitivity mode as it shot out into the depths of space in a straight line, a non-Euclidean straight line which travelled like Einstein surfing on a wave of light, transfixing the immensity of the universe until it came at last in no time at all in a grand grave circle to rest at the back of his head, muffled in its dying spasm by the intimacy of his pillow.

That's how Hamish woke up on the morning of the Thylacine, and his first sensible thought was to recall the advice of the immortal Tommy Hafey over a cup of tea: "If you play from behind, you're either an idiot or a squib".

So Hamish leaped out of bed and attacked the day from the front like Jim Stynes. He did without breakfast because it was too early and he did without coffee or a nice Tommy Hafey cuppa because there wasn't any time. El Nino promised to make that day, already hot, a scorcher. Hamish jumped into his white van and got moving with the windows down to get a breeze ruffling what was left of his hair. He turned on the radio. In those days, before he discovered audio books, he liked to listen to ABC Classics because there was less talking and if there were lyrics they were unintelligible, either because they were in another language or because they were being sung by serious musicians trained in the Conservatorium to annunciate in such and such a way and let the audience read the surtitles. So there would be no annoying jibber jabber until midday when Margaret Throbsby (remember her?) would conduct her insipid interview. Sometimes Hamish fantasized about becoming a famous micro-biologist or a virtuoso cellist so he could be

invited onto Margaret Throbsby's program and choose the
five pieces of music that would best offend the outraged ABC
Classics audience. Liberace or the Sex Pistols? Kamahl or James
Last? N.W.A. performing Fuck the Police or Burt Reynolds
performing Ask Me What I Am? Gunter Noris, Horny Volume
1? What do you think?

I drove along in a pleasant daze. Hamish was sick of composing
this narrative in the third person. It was tiresome so I jumped
into an easygoing first person voice, as you see. I think I drove to
Wonthaggi but I might have gone to Korumburra or Leongatha
or Inverloch first. It's not important. It was a long time ago and
my memory is wonky. In fact, I am going to go to bed now
and tackle this narrative fresh in the morning, the way Jack
Kerouac might have done. I quite like Jack Kerouac, especially
since I listened to On The Road read by Matt Dillon. Matt does
a creditable Dean Moriarty, Yaaas, Yaaas! However, William S
Burroughs Jr was my hero back in the 1970s. Oh yes, bed.

I have had to break off this narrative while my sons and I await
the results of our auditions for Jesus Christ Superstar, next
year's big production of the Wonthaggi Theatrical Group. My
mood swings from elation and confidence through indifference
to shame and despair. It is quite unsettling and makes literary
composition impossible. It is, I imagine, how Schrodinger's Cat
must feel.

Elation and joy! We have all been given parts in JCSS. In the
ensemble. I can write again. That night I went to bed thinking of
Jack Kerouac whom I admire tremendously, not only because of
the speed at which he produced On The Road, but also because
of the way his entire body of work forms as it were a mighty

edifice much like a cathedral, with each portion contributing
in its allotted place to the magnificent whole. Thomas de
Quincey saw his life's work in this way. However my thoughts
soon turned to William S Burroughs Jr whose work appealed to
me for quite another reason. I was very taken with the cut-up
method, and the rationale behind it when I first discovered it at
University (not I hasten to add through the conservative syllabus
I was presented with, a syllabus that barely covered modernism,
let alone postmodernism or America even). All writers use
various methods to break through the veil of illusion which
separates us from the truth - drugs, alcohol, mystical techniques,
sex, dream journals, psychoanalysis, mortification of the flesh,
pipe smoking. Burroughs proposed a method by which he
could snatch a glimpse of the hidden reality lurking concealed
beneath the banal and everyday world of shimmering surfaces,
and get to grips with the cogs and gears which truly drive the
great machine of the world. I did many experiments of my own
with his cut-up method back then. After all it was great fun.
You can find some of these essays amongst my Selected Works.
No-one liked them at the time, in fact some people found them
offensive. They were universally rejected by the literary journals
to which I offered them. In fairness to my critics, even I did not
see what these poems were really all about - premonitions of
Princess Diana, the Twin Towers, the death of Superman, the
rise of Max Gawn, COVID 19, the apotheosis of Rose Hancock -
but now the method is demonstrably vindicated. Cut-up created
gaps in the fabric of reality through which the truth and the
real, the past and the future can slip to and fro, invisible and yet
palpable, much as the Thylacine seems to be able to do.

On that morning, the morning of the Thylacine, I switched the
radio from the classics to the cricket. Has anyone else ever noticed

the equivalence of Test Cricket and Wagner's Ring Cycle? I had always sensed it without pinning it down in sharp focus until the first day of the Third Test of the Ashes summer of 2013/14 which started in Perth and so was three hours behind the Eastern states. The last session was going to clash with the final performance of Melbourne's Ring - Gotterdamerung. What to do? I was torn between two lovers but in the end I went with Wagner, and it was then that I noticed that both cricket and Wagner are interminably long, both feature recurring leitmotifs, prolonged periods of inexorably rising tensions, moments of high drama, acts of passion, stupidity and vengeance, great heroes, evil villains, superior creatures of lofty arbitrariness and impartiality, and they both leave their audience physically and emotionally drained, yet craving more, a bit like mogadons in the old days. Next time you watch the cricket, put on the Ring of the Nibelungs instead of Richie Benaud and see if it makes more sense.

This narrative ground to a halt many years ago due to the distractions of the Pipe Smoking Authors project which occupied my attention for the past ten years. For a long time I thought I could incorporate the pipe smokers into this text, but now that there are over 1350 listings in the ghastly cortege of pipe smoking authors, they deserve their own monograph. I am a university graduate - surely I can solve an inconsequential problem like that and keep the two projects apart

And so, the Thylacine. Later that day, the day of the Thylacine, I was driving home from my pressing business in Wonthaggi, my attention divided between the radio and the empty road that stretched out before me. Not far from home I came into a long stretch of road, about a kilometre long and dead straight. Far ahead I saw what I took to be a large dog, crossing the road with a peculiar loping gait. I remember thinking " there's a naughty dog slinking away from some bad behaviour" and I was struck more and more by its strange slow walk. As I drew nearer I saw that its back legs moved together in a hopping motion while its front legs walked in a more dog like march. I saw its strangely tapering tail, fat at the rump and extending straight behind in an unusual way for a dog. By the time I drew level with the animal it was standing in the roadside vegetation looking back at me over its shoulder and it wasn't until then that I saw the stripes across its back. It looked at me full in the face with its wide catlike eyes and its small catlike ears, and as I rushed by at a sensible 95 kph, I realised at once that it was a thylacine. It was broad daylight, I hadn't touched a drop all day, I was in full control of my faculties - there could be no doubt, it was a thylacine. There was an instant of crypto-communication between us as our eyes met, two sentient beings on this tiny orb, a marble, spinning like a coin on a polished hardwood floor, careening around the Milky Way towards its cataclysmic appointment with Andromeda in five or six billion years. And then, I continued on my way and all I thought was "How interesting, a thylacine".

When I tell this story to city folk, even Melburnians, they always look at me as though I had told them I was abducted by aliens. After all, the consensus of scientific thought is that the thylacine is extinct, and anyway, it was only ever to be found on Tasmania. When I tell other members of the Trumble family they are naturally polite, as I would expect. But when I tell my neighbours in South Gippsland, they usually have seen a thylacine themselves, often more than once, often more than one. There are two schools of thought on how it is that the thylacine comes to call South Gippsland, especially the

Wonthaggi Triangle, its habitat. The first is that the thylacine has always been here, sheltered in the impenetrable temperate rainforest which even today is to be found in remnant pockets in the steep and lonesome gullies which the farmers who own them never visit. The fossil record of the thylacine tells us that once it roamed all across the Australian mainland and even the jungles of Papua New Guinea. The steel trap minds of scientists maintain that the beast is extinct - where, they say, is the evidence of their survival outside Tasmania, and not there either. Well, I am evidence because I have seen one. Also note, South Gippslanders are leery of broadcasting their thylacine sightings because there are some people, hunters, publicity seekers, crypto-zoologists, who want nothing better than to be the one who killed the last remaining thylacine - where are *they* to be found? At or around the latest reported sighting. The second school of thought suggests that when it became apparent that the thylacine was being driven to extinction in Tasmania by hunters, pastoralists and hydro electric engineers, in the 1930s, a group of concerned environmentalists secretly released breeding pairs on the mainland, some say on Wilson's Promontory, others on the shores of Westernport Bay. We know the same thing was done for koalas when their numbers shrank on the mainland from loss of habitat, and a colony was successfully established on Phillip Island. Either way, there is no doubt that small groups of thylacine continue to thrive in my neighbourhood.

But the thylacine endures in more than the physical manifestation l encountered on that scorching summer day (I believe my thylacine broke cover searching for a drink). Oh yes, the thylacine pervades the zeitgeist of our times, it festers in the secret fantasies of every woman, child and man, it is implicit in every manifesto from Dada and the Futurists, to Postmodernism and Post structuralism, from anarchism to Gaia, from Ruskin's Pathetic Fallacy to anti-speciesism, from Keats' Negative Capability to Bodyline. Its platonic form has weaselled its way into my dreams, my thoughts, my belief system, my DNA probably, my very heart. And the meaning of the thylacine? Its mission? Its purpose? Its legacy? What does the Thylacine say?

(Actually, the call of the thylacine is often mistaken for the desperate scream of a woman in distress, something to give anyone the heebie jeebies in the middle of a cold bleak night.)

Epilogue

Thylacine stalks the dainty does in the Highland pine forests, they roam the frozen deserts of Patagonia with the ghosts of Butch and Sundance and Macro the Wonderdog. They circle the wary badger in its midnight frolics, they scale the desolate high passes to Shangri-La. They snigger at the knuckleheads in their manky suits in the crumbling CBDs of the West. At night, they lurk in the significant roadside vegetation along the back roads of South Gippsland, flushing out rabbits into the path of oncoming traffic and retrieving the kill once the speeding utes are out of sight. They scuttle across the Arctic seabed with the pink starfish and the white spiders beneath the solid ice above them and cunningly avoid the cameras of the BBC frogmen sent out on their perilous quest by Sir David Attenborough. Pliny the Younger reported scores of thylacine swimming out to sea on the morning of 23 August CE 79. The thylacine has mastered flight by an algorithm which tallies their lift and thrust and ensures the sum exceeds their drag and that bastard gravity. Thylacines marched with Napoleon's conquering Grande Armee from Austerlitz to Jena. And they have evolved the power of cloaking themselves with selective invisibility through the application of Mind. And they have mastered space flight by rejecting the tin can approach of NASA and embracing the inner route to the stars. They rub their flanks on the ancient standing stones in Languedoc, graveyard of the Cathars. Thylacines are the secret sponsors of the movement for perpendicular interment. "Champagne, champagne for everyone", they cry in the Casino at Monte Carlo. Thylacines stood in the crowd of fawning courtiers who cruelly mocked the frenzied buffoon Rigoletto in his misery. They fasten their seatbelt securely during periods of turbulence over the Charlie Gibbs Fracture Zone sipping an Aperol spritz in the cocktail lounge of their 747, they slip silently in pairs along the cobbled lanes of Paris and Glasgow, they move backwards and forwards along the continuum of time simultaneously like Merlin. Thylacines are to be found in the Army of Shadows of the secret Bizango cult responsible for voudu zombification on Haiti. Their aura vibrates with the disembodied hum of sub atomic particles in the inner workings of the Machine that watches us all, victim or perpetrator, every hour of every day. I saw a thylacine drinking a pina colada in Trader Vic's. They never lose their temper when they get in a barroom fight. What is their prey? It is you, my dearies, in the Jason recliners of your oblivion, it is you in the airport on Saturday, it is you my sweetie in this case of bananas you call the office and it is you when you least anticipate the boys will have the opportunity.

The thylacine watched from the shadows as the terrible vengeance of Truganini was wrought upon her whaler rapist on the beach at Cape Paterson. Two lovers kiss in the window of a fashionable cafe, unaware of the steady gaze of the thylacine from the shadows outside, or are they? Another nail salon opens up on the High Street. Coincidence? I think not, thinks I. The thylacine hunts you within the secret subterranean cities of the Old World and the neon glow of godforsaken New World urban wastelands. It is you, mon vieux, the thylacine hunts, their nostrils aquiver with your degenerate odour. The thylacine theirself has a curious scent - the Portuguese have a word for it: "Saudade". The presence of absence. Thylacine exudes a profound melancholy, longing for the thing that is gone, lost, perhaps we might even think extinct. Certainly the scientific mind is seduced by this ploy. The scientist disrespects the thylacine, like the last tooth in an old man's mouth - there is nothing to work with. The superior man stands in awe of the thylacine.

The thylacine's return heralds the end of our world, the death of humanity, the extinction of man. Thylacine knows the secret passage out of the Underworld, knows too the secret of Orpheus and his heavy metal guitar - Don't look back. Humanity bobs up and down on the ocean swell of eternity, its anchor snagged in the sandy white rocks of Reason below while a tremendous deadly tidal wave of Love approaches.

MY COFFIN

That night I didn't sleep at all.
I was high over the earth
Many kilometres high as it happens
On an overnight flight
From Singapore to Melbourne
And I dosed myself liberally
With complimentary champagne
For you see I was travelling
Business class.
The sweet flight attendant
Incorrigible Pollyanna of sedulity
Turned my seat into a bed
So I could lie down with a blankie
And a pillow.
Go to sleep...go to sleep...
As we natives say "fa subito"
But I am a tall man
A natural born Lurch
And the business class bed
Forced me into an awkward S-bend

On my less favoured side
So I couldn't sleep.
I lay there for hours
Trying not to think about a tin box
Hurtling through the ice cold stratosphere
Consuming finite resources
In a world spiralling into climate crisis
So my thoughts turned instead -
Due to my awkward confinement -
To my coffin.
When the time comes
Would they make for a big fat tall man like me
Qua corpse
A bespoke coffin to fit
Or would they stuff me into one off the shelf
As cramped as the driving seat
Of the Nissan Navara?
Would my plus size cause difficulties
For the coffin bearers?
Or the hearse?
Or at the Crematorium?
I hope they don't chop my feet off
And put them neatly shod
By my side. I hope they don't
Break my legs and shunt them
Up and to the side to fit me in
Last season's coffin on special.
I am supposing I will go into a coffin
Prior to the oven
Because I have left no instructions
About my terminal wishes, such as
A foetal position pod beneath a pear tree

Or a sailor's burial at sea
Or perpendicular interment
Or a sky burial like what they do in Tibet
But I am reluctant to specify
Being squeamish
So I don't think about the housekeeping of Death
Except when I can't sleep on a plane
And I'm too polite to disturb others
Watching a movie which would no doubt
Make me laugh out loud.
Like Deadpool and Wolverine did.
Especially the grave side fight
With the adamantium body parts
Which reminds me of my own
Vibranium skull implants
And what will become of them
In the crematorium furnace.
Later on I asked my dentist.
He, bemused,
Said no-one had asked him that before
But he supposed the titanium posts
Would resist melting
Like steel plates and pins
Or cobalt-chromium hip joints
But not perhaps gold teeth.
Are they valuable these titanium pieces?
And could they be reused?
Could they be sold
To unscrupulous businessmen
Or ghoulish body snatchers
Could they be pawned on the dark web
Could they be crafted into a pair of earrings

A charming Memento Mori
For a favourite goddaughter
Or a daughter-in-law?
Every time I have handled the ashes
Of a dear departed
They always consist only of the finest ash
With no bits and bobs
As if they had been sifted
Passed through a very fine sieve.
Hmmmm...
Rem acu tetigisti!
Undertakers! J'accuse!
But wait!!
A new development.
I crave affection baby but not when I drive.
Now the tungsten implant
Has fallen out with me.
My dentist warned me at the outset
One in twenty will not take
But now it appears that I misheard him
And it's one in five.
So now my skull has an empty plughole
Which needs plugging with a bone graft
Ah, the vicissitudes of teeth!
But no procedure could be simpler
I'm told
For the bone they use is not my own
But a granulated product pre-prepared
Where from? I naturally ask
Passing up the chance to say "Whence?"
Not wishing to appear a ponce.
A mumbled sheepish devoiced reply before

My mouth is quickly disabled
With clamps and swabs and needles.
Later when Doctor has retired
To his lair
And the surging swell of his mighty Wurlitzer
Echoes along the corridor
I ask again his assiduous assistant
Who reluctantly tells me the bone is
"Bovine"
Not ovine, for that would be a sheep
Not porcine, for that would be a pig
Not aquiline, for that would be an eagle.
No.
Bovine, of, or pertaining to, a cow
Or perhaps a buffalo
Or bison, or oxen
Or perhaps a bull
But probably from a cow.
Lucky I'm a pescatarian,
A vegaquarian,
Goodness knows what might ensue
Were I to eat beef now.
Holy Cow, Batman
My superhero back story has begun
And I await with avidity
My new superpowers
Will my bovine senses tingle
Like Friendly Neighbourhood Spiderman's?
Will I transform into a raging bull
With every china shop visit
Or stock market mention
Like Incredible Hulk?

Will my legal DNA, long dormant,
Awake and blossom me into a new career
Like She-Hulk, Attorney at Law?
Will I communicate telepathically with my cow subjects
Like Aquaman and his fish?
Or will I shapeshift from my true cow form
Like J'onn J'onzz, the Martian Manhunter?
Will I ride with my stampeding herd into battle
Like Astonishing Ant-Man?
All day
I graze
Through the fridge
And the pantry
And the larder
And the milkbar
And the cafe
And the sushi palace
And the bottle shop
And settle down
And chew my cud
And fall asleep
At last....

DEATH IN VENICE

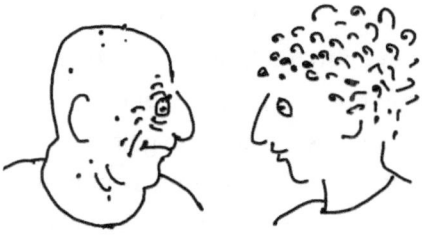

"Venezia - sara la mia fine..."

1.

Oh, Venice!
City of plumbers, and Nutella, and illusion,
The shimmering sweet glamour of mirage and deceit -
Where the Virgin might appear at any time
Disguised as a voluptuous blonde in a puffer jacket,
Or a gay gondolier in ribbons and plastic roses -
Where masks are all the same
Concealing all the same faces -
Where mirrors magnify the Liberace kitsch,
The evil worm gnawing within the lovely blossoms of art -
And the dogs prowl her slick stone streets
In chic designer overcoats
While their servile owners pluck up their shits
In Gucci baggies, outside the bijouteries,
Bombonieries,
Nicknackeries,
And the drowning tourists hold aloft their selfie sticks,
To drag a last glimpse of heaven down to hell,
Like Tashtego in his death gasp grasp,

The shrieking angelic bird pinned to the
mast of the doomed Pequod.
Oh Venice!
Your churches have no congregations
And your communists genuflect at Our Lady's Shrines -
No cars, no ants, no golf at all -
You make porcini mushrooms out of marzipan
And marzipan fruits out of glass
And pizzas out of Nutella -
You clean your streets with dishwashing liquid -
Palmolive green - Venice you're soaking in it -
Blue green algae stains your waters
The delicate colour of crysto-mint lifesavers -
Liquid crysto-meth for nostalgic baby boomers
In a lagoon without fish,
Tawdry Gippsland Lakes theme park
And the turtles refuse to escape Garibaldi's overflowing fountain,
Despite a clutter of cast off Nutella wrappings.
Nearby, rival maestros face off -
Wagner and his pelican, feeding his screeching children
With the blood of his beak-pierced bosom,
And Verdi and his trumpets announcing the Apocalypse
To a chorus in feathers and pink tights -
Do they climb down from their midnight plinths
To scratch each other's eyes out?
Oh Venice!
Proclaiming the death of the Architect -
Read the bereavement notice in the Guttenberg Press -
With nothing left to show except
Rococo self-storage units filled with priceless, worthless art
Poised over a dank abyss
A death trap, a bottomless brunch in the Land of No Form.

2.

I wade through the receding tide in my gumboots
Behind a young boy with impossibly curly hair,
Just like mine was,
Tall and stooped like me
Hands clasped behind our backs,
He turns
Our eyes meet infinitesimally briefly and
I see myself in the strange mirror of time
And then he is gone and I search the crowd in vain.
It was me. Young me. Teen me. 1975 spunky me.
My corduroy flares and desert boots flood ruined.
Did I notice elderly me then? I don't remember,
Sloshing down that sodden lane across the gulf of generations.
But why should I have noticed then
An elderly gent, elderly me,
Having-let-myself-go me.
Recognition belongs to the glassy side of the mirror
And Dorian Gray's portrait stares at its
subject with sightless eyes
And that moment is gone -
A D.H. Lawrence moment,
Imperceptible yet palpable,
An inchoate moment without dimensions,
The moment one falls into a chrono-synclastic infundibulum,
A still point.
The ribbon at Olympia's throat.
A witch's boat of clipped fingernails.
A Bridge of Sighs -
Foolproof escape route for Casanova
And Cagliostro,

And all the rest.
The tear at the corner of Melania's nose.
The Nutella smudge on Peggy's pouting mouth.
Socrates said that the Poet draws inspiration from the gods
and yet rarely becomes fully and painfully
aware of the irrelevance
and social impotence of the poet's art.
This moment of connection was just such an occasion.
The floor sways beneath my sea legs
Still at sea in too many rooms
My arms around too much stuff
My useless fantome wings unfurled in vain
Like Cassandra setting all the clocks wrong and unsynchronized
Like Echo raising her stock above the coming king tide
Like Orpheus incanting the misery of the nobility -
Nutella on crepes,
Nutella injected mainline into croissants,
Nutella candied almonds,
Nutella just on its own, straight from the pot,
Serenissimma Nutellissima.

THE QUEEN

Oh The Queen!
You have let down at last your lovely hair
From the locked room
High in the dark tower
And Death has clambered up
To break open the shackles
The pinky shackles that match your hat
The iron shackles of duty you have worn
Since you were a wee lassie
And Death has freed you
Like Samson chained in the Temple
Given by Death the strength to die
Between twin pillars Church and State -
Or like Andromeda chained to the throne rock
Our sacrifice, we offered you up
To propitiate the sea monster dragon -
Released by Perseus Death -
But wait,
Were you not also the Dragon itself
Coiled upon your immense ill-gotten horde
Thy choicest gifts in store

Fouling the treasure with your exudations,
Were you not the Eye of the Dragon
The ever-open watchful keen one
Jealous of all the sundries
Who would plunder your booty
And loot their inheritance back?

Oh Lizard Queen
Return to your people beneath the earth
Victorious

Oh Queen Mab
Holding your tiny court in my CPAP palace
And every night you'd ride
Your unimaginable chariot
Along the pipe and up my nose
To sprinkle your coruscating fancies
Upon my oyster brain.
But now go tell the bees
You've left me for your Hellboy lover

Oh Borg Queen
Assimilation complete

Oh Glorious Boadicea
Battle-scarred Britannia
Defending our laws
Hmmm....

Oh Acid Queen
Don't remember much about you
Your Silver Jubilee
Whoa ..... silver, man,

Rainbow vampires and unicorns
With alablaster teeth
Late nights scoring in Soho
Bad boys in London Town
Punks along the King's Road
Biba's closing sale, IRA bombs,
Heavy

Oh Drag Queen
You go girl
In your colours
Of Dayglo Yellow
Like a field of rape in the sunshine
Of Lilac to Mauve
Like a gully choked with Paterson's Curse
Of Minty Green
Like a bastard man in white
In an outfit by Leigh Bowery
In a portrait by Rolf Harris
You go, bee atch

Oh Bandit Queen
Taking from the rich
Or something something
Cavorting in your highland fastness
With your band of men in garters,
(I stand confounded)
Merry no longer

Oh Virgin Queen
More chaste than any nun
Object of the impious lusts

Of all the men from Cowes to Venus Bay
But I, only I, know of whom you think
When you close your eyes
For I can see inside your head

Oh Gypsy Queen
Your mad majestic tarantella is done.
Hang up your tambourine
And leave your golden earrings
To the Archbishop of Canterbury

Old Mrs Batchelard
My razor strop toting Grade 5 teacher
Made me write "Noblesse Oblige"
One hundred times on the blackboard
A proto-upper-middle-class Bart.
That was my Quasimodo year
Ringing in the changes in the old bell tower.
The old Battleaxe didn't tell me what it meant
But you did Queenie, in Spades

When I was a child
A young Elizabethan
You were ever there
A superhero alter ego of my mother

With dominion over all the seas and lands
From the frozen wastes of the North-west Passage
To the sweltering jungles in the dark heart of Africa
And with the power of Corgi speech
Over the Christmas airwaves

Your orb her dinner bell
Your sceptre her wooden spoon
Your crown her Sunday bonnet

Like you she had four bairns
The well-beloved first born,
The sporty one, the posh one,
The brainy one, the naughty one,
The butch one, the girlie one,
The favourite one (that was I)
The senior management one,
The poppinjay, the doormat,
The martinet, the clothes horse,
The flibbertigibbet, the dolt,
And the one who ran away
To join the poetry circus

She was stern but loving
And though she loved us all equally
I knew she loved me best

Now she is gone and so are you,
Oh Pearly Queen, Oh Queen of the May.
Truly orphaned, motherless,
Abandoned in the forest
I must thrive

MY SHOP

I call my shop "The Penis"
because the suggestion of sex boosts sales.

I call my shop "The Christmas Penis"
so the customers know I carry giftware.

I call my shop "The House of the Christmas Penis"
in order to convey a sense of dignity.

I call my shop "The House of the Christmas Penis of Aphrodite"
for the cult of beauty is our stock in trade.

I call my shop "The House of the Christmas
Penis of Aphrodite Frock Salon"
because we sell frocks.

THE SONG OF THE LOBSTER

"Live lobsters hermetically sealed in cans
are now available to the housewife who wants her seafood fresh."
Advertisement in Popular Mechanic, February 1953.

Spacemen mince across the moon
They took their tea & a TV set.
World War III began too soon
But no one will admit it yet.

Lobsters locked in module cans
Every housewife Nixon scheming
Giant step for lobster man
Onto your plate fresh & screaming

MACRO THE WONDERDOG

Who Was Macro the Wonderdog?

Macro was a small black dog that came into my life when I took up with my then new girlfriend Maxine. A Kelpie cross. A wonderfully independent creature who roamed free and widely, finding alternative families to cadge food from, friendly butchers good for a chop, small children who could persuade their parents to visit her and give her attentive pats. I was not a very responsible pet owner.

When a man sits in his shop for many years, staring out at the street, a man might think he is standing still, going nowhere, while the street outside is in constant motion. The street is life itself it seems - meetings and partings, comings and goings, transactions and ditherings, success and failure, love and hate, joy and misery, lovers kissing and quarrelling, crowded trams rattling back and forth, buying and selling, selling and buying, thieves, beggars, junkies and drunks, a small black dog trotting up and down the footpath or sunning herself in the gutter - all parading before the stationary man in his bogged down shop, like a beached whale, Robinson Crusoe cast up on a desert island. Or so it would seem. You might think the sun revolves around the earth, because that is what it looks like. But we know, don't we, that the sun does not revolve around the earth, despite appearances. It is the earth that revolves. Nevertheless, it looks like the sun is spinning around the earth. But what should it look like for us to say, yes, it looks like the earth itself is spinning around the sun? This is a question famously posed long ago by Ludwig Wittgenstein, the gay icon, in a dusty Cambridge lecture theatre. I know because I am brainy and I read books. The answer of course is that it must look precisely as it does in fact, and we need to smarten up and open our eyes to the wonder of our own reality. The same is true of the street. And so it was that the man in his shop was not stationary at all, but incrementally going all over the place. And one direction he, that is to say, I, was headed was close on the heels of Macro the Wonderdog, as she propelled herself to stardom.

Every town has a certain dog who is the epicentre and focus of the adoration of doggie people, lonely guys, bag ladies, mobility scooter riders, soft hearted promenadiers, window lickers and flaneurs. Wonthaggi has Basil. Inverloch has Angus. Fitzroy was blessed with Macro the Wonderdog until her death in 1996, around the same time as the birth of Number One son. Coincidence? Yes? No? We will never know. She is buried at a secret location with her costumes, her props, the accoutrements of her craft and her theatrical notices, so archaeologists of the future will dig her up like Richard III and Attila the Hun, and marvel.

Macro's first appearance was in the following script. She went on to appear in numerous shows during the heady renaissance of comedy cabaret in Melbourne in the 80s. Her apotheosis came when she led the Brunswick St Parade as Queen of the Fringe. Several noses were put out of joint. Good!

A DOG IN THE MANGER

A Christmas Tableau Vivant first performed at The Prince
Patrick Hotel on Xmas Eve, 1984, with the following cast:
Joseph - The Magnificent Hamish
The Virgin Max - Maxine Macdonald
Macro the Wonderdog - Herself
Barman of the Inn - Some Dude
Archangel Debriel - Madame Deb (International Clairvoyant)
Wise Guys - Tim Smith etc
Animals, Shepherds - Drunken Patrons
Narrated by John Ashton, the Bard of Fitzroy

And it came to pass
In the Reign of Hawke,
A great census was decreed
And each must travel
To somewhere else
To be counted and photographed
And issued with an I.D. card.

So Joseph
(Tradition has it that he was the tallest)
ENTER JOSEPH
And his lady wife the Virgin Max
Who was big with dog at the time
ENTER VIRGIN MAX BIG WITH DOG

Set out for a pub in Collingwood.
THEY HIT THE BAR
But there was no room at the bar
"Thou mayest passeth the night on the stage
Amongst the performers and other animals"
Quoth the barman.
THEY HIT THE STAGE

And there they laid the new born dog
Wrapped in swaddling tinsel
In a lowly manger
STICK DOG IN MANGER
"AHHH"
FRIEZE

And the animals on the stage
All gathered about
In awed and reverent silence.
ENTER ANIMALS

And upon a green hill far away
Without the city walls of Collingwood
It was at a laundromat in Fitzroy
Some shepherds sat washing their socks
ENTER SHEPHERDS
But Lo!!!
The archangel Debriel came unto them
As in a vision
ENTER DEBRIEL
"Arise" she cried, "and follow me,
For this day is born a dog this day.
Come ye and adore her

For she is adorable, is she not?"
"AHHH"
FRIEZE

And from the Eastern Suburbs
Came Three Wise Guys
Smoking Camels
ENTER WISE GUYS
THEY CRACK SOME WISECRACKS
YUK YUK YUK
And they bore gifts
Of precious Pal
And a stick
And verily a tennis ball
To lay at the feet of the infant dog
"AHHH"
FRIEZE

We shall now sing Hymn No 12 345 678910
Maestro if you please

ALL SING
A dog in the manger
No fleas in her bed
The little dog Macro
Lay down her black head

The stars in the bright sky
Look down where she lay
ALL WHIP OUT GOLDEN STARS
OF STURDY CARDBOARD
WITH PAINTED EYES
AND HOLD THEM ALOFT

They said to Lord Macro
JOSEPH SINGS
Stay, Macro, Stay!!!!
ALL: AHHHH LE LU YAH

Let the Word go out
That God so loved the World
She sent her only begotten dog
To be a light in the darkness
With her message of Peace
And Goodwill to all species
And a happy Xmas to one and all
From Macro the Wonderdog
EXEUNT IN A NICE PROCESSION

MACRO THE WONDERDOG'S DREAM

Every day Macro The Wonderdog lies asleep in the gutter under the hot Fitzroy sun with only the twitching of her muzzle and her whimpering sighs to tell her passing fans she is not dead. Respectfully they hurry by, not wishing to disturb the artist at rest, and only a few ever wonder what visions, what fancies enliven the sleep of such a dog.

Macro The Wonderdog has only one dream. She dreams she is in South America. Boldly she roams the frozen deserts of Patagonia, baying at the headless giants across the straits of Magellan on Tierra Del Fuego, and chasing the god-forsaken albatross along cliffs of guano that plunge 200 feet into the Roaring 20s, until it is time to take coffee on the grand boulevards of Buenos Aires. Later she will dance the sinful tango in the Italian Quarter with pomaded youths, strutting heirs to a legacy of machismo and the stiletto. In her dream she rides with wild gauchos across the pampas, twirling her bolos gaily above her head as her silver spurs clink and jingle from her Cuban heels, and peons, startled by the magnificence of her accoutrements and enthralled by the haunting music of her pipes of Pan, forget for a moment their hunt for her armadillo sisters.

In Montevideo, Macro pays her respects to the ghost of Le Comte de Lautremont, the grandfather of Surrealisme.

Macro The Wonderdog cannot abide the fascists of Paraguay, so her dream takes her instead to Chile – not the Chile of Generalissimo Pinochet and Alan Bond, but the beautiful Chile of Pablo Neruda who once so touched her heart when he said "I would do to you what Spring does to the blossom tree." Macro chooses to fly Air Chile, whose passengers greet each take-off with ecstatic applause, to Rapa Nui, Easter Island, where the monoliths grow sterner with each fresh French outrage in the Pacific.

Returning in her hot air balloon, as did those ancient Indians who carved out their geometrical riddles upon the Plains of Nazca, Macro lands in Bolivia where she must carry a knapsack stuffed with the worthless currency she receives in change for her mate tea, before she sets sail with the Bolivian Navy across Lake Titicaca and into old Peru. For now the clouded Andes call, as if from a previous life, and Macro The Wonderdog walks once again the Inca trail to Machu Picchu, her llamas laden with maize and coca leaves. Here she feels a presence, a guide, a teacher if you will – it is Shirley Maclean. Once many lifetimes ago Shirley and Macro were both high priestesses in a notorious Toltec dog cult, and their destinies have been entwined ever since.

But the dream state will not linger long on past glories – it sweeps her on to Columbia, ah Columbia, in search of El Dorado and the mountain warlords who control the pernicious drug traffic from their upland fastnesses. From her austere perspective, Macro The Wonderdog gazes out at the sybarites along the golden beaches of Venezuela where the palms whisper sweet words to a dog and the sound of calypso wafts on breezes redolent with Yankee gunsmoke across the Caribbean from Trinidad and Tobago and Jamaica. Macro would fain follow the gentle music north, even to Cuba, where every dog can read and write, for, almost alone of her generation, Macro still remembers Che, once glorious black sheep of the Argentine middle class who took up too briefly the torch of Freedom first lit in Caracas by Simon Bolivar, The Liberator; Oh Che, poor sad homophobe reading his butch guerrillas Robert Louis Stevenson bedtime stories in their steaming jungle bivouac while the CIA assassins slunk through the night. Oh Che, now nothing more than a mincing preening prancing puppet in the tawdry Broadway fodder of Andrew Lloyd Webber – anyway, a more insistent rhythm draws her south, to Rio, where it is Carnivale, Farewell Meat, and the streets are filled with Samba.

Swept up in the madness of the bossa nova, the dreaming dog is close to waking, but the mighty Amazon carries her up its unimaginable length to Manaus, where, lost in a wilderness infested with crocodiles and piranha, cougar and mosquito, pompous rubber barons built their Babylonian opera house and ladies send their dry cleaning to Paris. Now Macro The Wonderdog is close to her goal. Enlisting the ethereal aid of Princess Ubangi whose hands are encrusted with diamonds and whose entourage of pygmy warriors carry their blow darts dipped in curare, Macro assumes the mantle of a Zen conquistadore, born to impose her righteous will upon an entire continent.

With a copy of Howl in one hand and The Naked Lunch in the other, Macro follows the footsteps of William Burroughs Jnr, the noted drug addict and homosexualist, up the Orinoco, hacking her way past the vine-choked ruins of Mayan temples, (striving in vain to insert the blade of her penknife between the massive blocks), in search of Yage, the ultimate fix.

All dogs have a natural instinct to defend that which they perceive to be their own territory, say veterinarian authorities. For Macro The Wonderdog, siesta is over and the constant harassment of skate-boarders, postmen, police, beggars, real estate agents, debt collectors, shoplifters, drunks, old ladies on buggies, junkies and small children must be attended to with a nip in the heel. But there is a piece of property beyond this Brunswick Street of the Conscious she will exert all her energy and, if necessary, give up her very life to defend. It is the South America of her dreams.

THE MARRIAGE OF FINN MAC COOL: OR I SAW A HALF EATEN ORANGE TREE, AND IT WAS MY MOTHER

She won three thousand pounds and the hearts of her people
from an Irish twister, soft like the kiss of cream.
As the scum of gold is silver, so she found
pleasure, luxury and romance,
forbidden love smudged from winter tomes,
she, she, ignoring his work, rejecting his feelings
because shyness is only deceit dressed up in modesty.
He wished he were a farmer, cold, not icy,
simple, not foolish,
dour, using age old methods of understatement,
a shot in the arm for the bored,
the angry, the frustrated,
and herself he wished a floating ball
of stationary frills, Mona Lisa in the kitchen.
Indeed she planned to give up so much for marriage
in a thin white blouse like an astronaut,
naked with hope. His giant skeleton
would add substance to her dull sallow skin
and she might paint her catch puce or fuschia.
They, a winning combination, a new unit,

taking to massage in a glow of physical vigour,
taking to diet to enforce the laws of health,
taking to bush walk rambles on wild mountainsides
in fun gumboots and tracksuit pants, brash and cocky,
with his big reckless Irish buccaneer's grin,
taking to smell the roses in times of trauma
and calling doctors without delay.
Resentment smouldered over the new status –
nudging each other towards consolation
and facing up to a modest public servant's cottage,
very French, no jokes, no opinions,
shin splints for her artistry
and music for his runner's knee,
all colour clotted and skimmed off
leaving a man in a grey suit with a furled umbrella,
all circumstance conspiring to promote
this strange liaison, perfume wed to a paperweight,
deep plunging curtsies of merciless intimacy,
so much of beauty and grace adding charm to an affair
like a pain in the mouth.

What did she know of manners,
hit by depression and the panache of a new look?
What did he care,
except inasmuch as it brought new hope for the infertile?
They ate their meals in a green wood garden;
hunger was the first course, the next is war.

PORT MELBOURNE

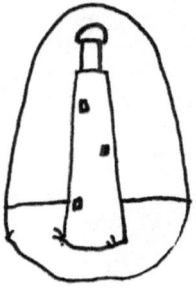

I like to live in Port Melbourne,
a country town in the inner urbs.
Fat streets and stumpy houses,
big stupid skies which grin like an idiot,
Clip clop milko at six o'clock,
shabby seagulls and kids with cricket bats,
aged neighbours who think we're married
a concrete boat in a rusty back yard
bluestone alleys and a railway track,
empty parks and sweet smelling factories,
a white lighthouse which can't see over the petrol tanks,
and everyone is leaving for the city.

TRAFFIC LIGHT

So, Traffic Light,
You caught me again
And here I stop, quivering, enraged,
Transfixed by your little arrows
Like Saint Sebastian,
Except he was LGBTQ as I take it.

No sense of humour, Traffic Light,
Too bossy for popularity,
A fine politician you would make.
Not.

Red and green would vibrate together pleasantly
But for your clammy amber compromise
And we, like flies preserved in Death,
Are rendered into antique curios.

Now stopping and starting are one
And I know the bondage of the electron.

LATIN RAP
(CATULLUS LI & LXXXV)

Latinism in Hellene affairs is almost always to be deplored.
P. Vellacott

PREAMBLE

In the year 62 BCE, the greatest city in the world was Rome, the bloated throbbing capital of a dying republic about to give birth to an empire which would stand for centuries as a wonder of the ages, where exquisite luxury rubbed shoulders with the most abject poverty, where grace and beauty were worshipped with the utmost savagery and cruelty, where stern and virtuous philosophers endured the jibes and cynicisms of libertines and mountebanks, where the odours of fish and urine hung in the air like a mist, where great men - Caesar, Pompey, Crassus, Cicero - circled each other warily, eyeing off the prize of absolute power, and into this stinking, glittering, oppressive, exhilarating, nauseating cesspool the hopeful masses flocked from the ends of the earth - among them a young man from the provinces with only his wits to commend him, seeking his fortune. Caius Valerius Catullus.

Two thousand years ago
No TV no Radio
No potatoes, no spaghetti,
No gay marriage, no confetti,
No big cars, no cigarettes,
No bananas, no regrets,
No rip-off Golden Airplane game,
Everything else was just the same.
The centre of the world - a town called Rome
A cat called Catullus called it home
Catullus rapped in ancient Latin
Came to town and threw his hat in
Put down poems as smooth as satin
Some of the poems must have been rotten
But they're the ones that were soon forgotten
The ones we have are all ripsnorters
Give no quarters
Lock up your daughters
Catullus hung with all they smarties
All they big fat arty farties
Went to all they dinner parties
Met the in crowd
The thin crowd
The all my life where you bin crowd
He fell in love with sweet Clodia
Off his brain with sex desire
She was famous for her looks
You look it up in the history books
That look in her eye that young men know
Cicero - he tells us so.
Shit girl
She was an It Girl

People said she fucked her brother
She said they just liked each other
The brother was a wheeler dealer
Scene stealer
Big risk taker, trouble maker
Muck raker, mover shaker,
Deal breaker
Coming from the ruling classes
Scratch they arses
Running with the gangsta crew
Who knew? Did you? Me too.
His sister was an operator
Heart palpitator
Heat generator
This chicky babe would be equated
Paparazzi correlated
Paris Hilton, Lady Gaga,
Fergie, Pink, yeah, what a saga
She was married but sophisticated
Catullus he got captivated
Infatuated
Really badly fascinated
They dated
He wrote love poems intoxicated
He found a Greek one, antiquated
One of Sappho's, love related
Sappho was a Lesbos rapper
No slapper
Toe tapper
(She was gay or so they say
It's not important either way)

The well to do and educated
Cultivated
Elevated
Emancipated
Knew they Greek prefabricated
So this fine poem he located
Technically quite complicated
Into Latin he translated
For Clodia pre-meditated
Breath bated
I found his and re-translated
Trade it for your lover's kiss
This one's hot and it goes like this:

Who's that homey, where's he at
Like sitting with her like just like that
Face to face and knee to knee
Eating cake with a cup of tea
Yak yak yak and sip sip sip
When I'm that close it makes me flip
See, she's so cool and she's so fine
Knocks me senseless, worse than wine
A tongue-tied tongue in a mouth of stone
I got a fire down deep in every bone
And when she laughs – can't hear a thing
Ears start ringing with an inward ring
And when she smiles better hold on tight
'Cause I lose my sight
Like it's the middle of the night
That's right
Alright
Time on your hands boy nothing to do

Too much time and nothing to do
Going stir crazy doing nothing
Huffing
Puffing
Wild and scraggy
Daggy, shaggy,
Sappy,
Crappy...
Get a grip, get a grip
This is the way the big men slip
This is the way the bad scenes flip
What a trip!

Odi et amo - I hate and I love
Odi et amo - I hate and I love
Want to know why?
I don't know
I only know
It's what I feel
Excruciated.

THE BALLAD OF A GOOD LOOKING MAN

Here I come. I'm swinging on down the street
I'm striding out. My head is high.
I'm grooving along with my head held high.
I believe I'm doing the Alexander Technique.
It helps me look this good.

Hey, you ladies in the beauty parlour
Having your nails done,
Check me out, shoulders back,
My head held high,
I'm a good looking man.

Hey, you cool cats at the Italian cafe,
Drinking another long macchiato,
Fagging on, playing bezique,
You'll never get as good looking as me,
Not with all those bad habits.

Hey, you junkies, get out of my way,
Go and clean someone's perfectly clean windscreen,
Or go and ask someone else for sixty cents,
I'm a good looking man and I'm coming through.

Hey, Mr Shopkeeper, sweep your footpath,
Sweep up all that stuff into the gutter,
All those ciggies, all those butts,
I'm a good looking man and my shoes are clean.

No thanks, Mr Beggar, I don't have any loose change for you
To catch a tram home again today
Or buy yourself a pie, as if,
I need every cent for myself, man,
Because I'm so good looking.

Hey, you Vietnamese dudes playing billiards,
Playing some kind of dominoes,
In your Vietnamese club there, what do you reckon?
Am I a good looking man or what?

I feel good in my snazzy duds;
I have self-esteem.
There's a spring in my step;
My body is a temple.
I can see the blue sky overhead
Through the spider web of power lines
I can feel the sun on top of my head;
It's that male pattern baldness.
Look out, motorists!
I'm crossing the street.
Look out, Mr Newsagent!
I want to buy The Age.
Look out, Mr Postie!
Don't give me any bills today.
Look out Mr Milk Bar Man
I'll have a blue heaven malted thanks.

Girls! How are you going?
Catch you later.

Hey, Mr Taxi Driver, get me out of here quick smart;
Hang a rightie, drop a leftie,
Do a Uie.
I'm a good looking man and I'm needed elsewhere.

And you listen to me, Mr Talkback Radio Host!
Who cares what you think anyway?
How good looking are you anyway?
Hiding away in snivelling Radioland.

Hello, friendly dogger, sniffing the dirty old pavement,
Mooching around your lonesome beat,
Scrounging around for one last chop.
A good looking man always has time for a friendly black dog.

Ho, you loony youth!
Lairising on the tramstop,
Skylarking on the tramstop,
A good looking man salutes you.

As for you, Mr Parking so called Officer,
You will never be good looking in your fascist uniform,
And a good looking man would rather go on the dole
Than do your crummy job.

Hey, check it out, I'm in the city,
I'm strutting around the dead heart of this town like a rooster,
Like a true dinks peacock,
And I'm looking good;
I'm looking as good as Marcello Mastroianni,
I'm at least as good looking as Hugh Grant,

I'm just as good looking as Marcello Mastroianni,
Man, I'm as good looking as Dermie!

You know it,
I know it
Why deny it?
I'm a good looking man.

THE PROPER JESUS
11/12/09

Mum is with Jesus now - I am certain of that. I only hope she has found the right Jesus. There are a great many Jesuses, you know - Roman Catholic Jesus, Jewish Jesus, Greek Orthodox Jesus and Coptic Jesus; clean shaven Jesus and beardy Jesus (there is however no mustachioed Jesus) Muslim Jesus, Mormon Jesus, Quaker Jesus, and Uniting Church Jesus; teetotal Jesuses and Jesuses who drink, Jesuses who use mind altering substances; celibate Jesuses and monogamous Jesuses and free love swinger Jesuses under the sign of the Pineapple; carnivorous and vegetarian and vegan and gluten-free and omnivorous Jesuses and Jesuses with all manner of dietary prohibitions; black Jesus, Hindu Jesus and lesbian Jesus. Bi Jesus, trans Jesus and gay Jesus. Some Jesuses are easy to pick and steer clear of: Russian Jesus likes to wear a lot of bling, Pentecostal Jesus has fits of gibberish, Methodist Jesus, well, say no more, Amish Jesus and his funny beard. Some Jesuses will be hard for you and me to differentiate, like the various Anglican Jesuses, some of which or whom look just like Roman Catholic Jesus (although not Jesuit Jesus or Christian Brother Jesus) and some are more like your Presbyterian Jesus. Not your Methodist Jesus. Some Jesuses like to pass rattlesnakes around. A lot of American Jesuses like to carry firearms because it is his constitutional right. Some Jesuses like selfies and some frown on portraits of any kind. Some Jesuses like to be called Jesu and some prefer Christ Almighty, some Jesuses are the Messiah and some are not, some Jesuses are going to come again and some have already been and gone already. Some Jesuses go around all on their own and some have huge entourages of Saints and Disciples and little children. Some Jesuses wear a halo, some wear an uncomfortable looking crown of thorns, and some have what looks like a tattoo of a bleeding heart on their chest. Most Jesuses sport a lovely robe, and some favour a smart three piece business suit, except when they get nailed up on their various crosses when they generally go in for a discreet loin cloth. And then there's the Mother – don't get me started. Wevs, I hope MY mother has hooked up with her own proper Jesus and he has finally put her right about what's really happening, baby.

IRONING THE HANKIES

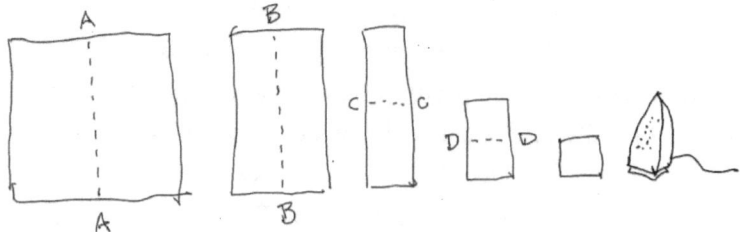

Oh labour of Sisyphean futility!
How many years since I,
An idle husband of a loving wife,
Last ironed my hankies?
But now today I will turn this crumpled heap
Into a smart spanking tribute
To Politenessman.
It was Auntie Anne who first taught me
To iron the hankie
Stern Amazon of Armadale
Sapphic manipulator
Prickly stickler for the form of the norm
And I a little boy
Bewildered by the company of women
Eating raw eggs and dripping
While Mum and Dad, kids agisted,
Toured France from Champagne
To the French Riverina
In a haze of garlic and vin du pays,
Taking in le striptease
Le plus sexy de Paris.

Where did Auntie get all those gentleman's hankies?
I suppose she kept them in her trouser pockets.
Later she even paid me to iron Uncle Henry's
But that was after the first lavender marriage was called off
And here came Henry with his cravats and cigarette holder
Proudly vaunting his diet of steak and Mars Bars
Drunk again on whisky
Singing Basin Street, Doo De Doo,
And banging the table
While Auntie disguised his greens
(Vegetable muck)
In a gravy puree.
Oh Hankie!
The gentleman's palimpsest
Of sweat, phlegm, blood, semen and tears,
So many moments of pain and joy,
Misery and exultation,
Desolation and ecstasy,
Smoothed over, over and over,
Folded and threadbare,
Cotton older than me, older than Gandhi,
Here's a Cash's label Mum sewed on the corner
It's my brother's
Here's one of mine, monogrammed "H"
Another red herring from the Orient Express
And did Auntie Anne have a girlie hankie
Pixies and toadstools
Butterflies and bouquets
Or was it a dirty big manly man's one
Neatly stashed in her handbag that day
When she came to watch me play soccer
For Jesus Thirds

Nick Hornby on the wing
Standing in the driving rain on the sidelines
Bellowing "Come on, Jesus,
Get stuck into them, Jesus"
At the top of her voice, so happy,
Ferocious Myrmidon maiden,
Valkyrie virgin, wielding her razor sharp wit,
Honed to a tingling edge
By years of bitter disappointment,
As she rode too soon
Into the golden twilight of Walhalla

PLANTATION

Pine trees placed in rows will grow
Into a neon green shag pile swathe
Like wads of money
Or Harry Beitzel's hair.
Should we take a wabi sabi leaf
From the Japanese gardener
And take the natural untamed beauty
Of our own inscrutable inheritance
But make it more beautiful
With geometrics of pine?
With an underlay of needles
No boisterous bouncing natives will disturb
The serene rustle of these exotic trees
Turning in nebulous metamorphosis
From a landscape of lacquered veneer
To woodchip heaps
To oriental houses of taste
Leaving no sign
But an A bomb aesthetic of death
And a residue of dollars

NOUVELLE CALEDONIE NOCTURNE

"The only church that illuminates is a burning church"
Buenaventura Durutti

Come let us stroll down to the heart of town
Bearing our gifts to neo-colonialism
- sledging
- ball tampering
- post-dated cheques
- offshore detention
And lay them in the Square Orly
A tribute to Jean-Baptiste Orly, Governor,
Pointing one way, gazing at something else
And each passer-by's "Bonjour"
A whispered kiss lip blown for me.
No such courtesy for you
Great High Kanak Chief Atai,
Your righteous revolt crushed beneath
That iron gubernatorial boot heel -
A trick learned at Sagallou, Djibouti, 1889,
When his furious cannonade
Dislodged the Russians from their fort,
Cossacks and bearded monks

Cold steel and icons
Sapristi! Scampering about
Like bullants flushed from a nest
And earning him a Pacific posting,
Tiptoeing among the mother-of-pearl yabbies
The coral growing beneath his skin
Like an idea fixe
The girls smelling of coconut and barbe de papa
Fairy floss at an all-you-can-think buffet
And postmodern tattoos in the place
Of incredulity towards the metanarrative
Tricolores gai peeping through the palms
And the Coconut Squad scooting up the trunks
With a dirty big machete
Patrolling prophylactically
Against the fate of Arnold Ehret
Whose mucusless diet was powerless
To prevent a fatal coconut dropping on his head
The faint roar of the reef hidden in the mist
Where the English fish absorb their toxins
And Napoleon III raised his pre-fab Pharos
And further out where arcane currents
And wheeling stars
And seagulls and turtles
Carry the news to Pablo Neruda.
It was the mountains rising out of the sea
That brought Scotland to the questing restless mind
Of Captain Cook, conquistadore ingles,
But it was the decadent tones of Debussy and Ravel
That would trill down the glens,
The skirl of ukuleles not bagpipes
Not Burns but Hugo,

The Ghost of Gauguin, not RLS's.
Great Orly told Atai
Who complained that French cattle
Were trampling the taro crops,
To put up fences.
Great Atai told Orly
He would put up fences
When his taros took to trampling the French cattle.
Orly sent in the army
Orly sent Atai's severed head to Paris.

It was Max Weber
Who observed that the Frenchie
Is an animal suspended
In webs of significance
He himself has spun.

THE LOVE SONG OF CAGLIOSTRO
AND MACRO THE WONDERDOG

She flits through the night on bat wings of flight
Straight to the hall where her ancestors dwell
She rides like a steed on hooves shod with speed
That clatter on flint in the courtyards of Hell.

She lopes under moonlight a wolf in her stealth
Stalking her prey by its innocent smell
She lurks in the shade of cathedrals of wealth
And her eye gleam haunts merchants who buy just to sell

She dances the polka, she dances the waltz
She tangos and flings her corsage to the floor
How irksome it seems when her partner proves false
She spurns his attentions and shows him the door

The bright comet shoots across ten million stars
Its omen is read in the temples of Rome
They throw him in prison, he slips through the bars
For destiny calls him inexorably home

Cagliostro, Cagliostro, I hear of you sung
In the song of the porpoise, the scream of the swallow
The spider has finished devouring her young
The old world must die for a new world to follow

Two lovers kiss in a cabriolet
Two candles burn with one searing flame
Two hearts beat out a tattoo too fey
Time and space echo with each whispered name

FROM MY DESK IN HEAD OFFICE OF THE DEFENCE DEPARTMENT

You are my sticky tape dispenser
Fixing me with your solidity
To the desk top of life
And measuring out the Durex of my desire

You are my Westgate Bridge
Opening up the western suburbs of my heart
For the land deals of love

You are my executive model calculator
Reconciling the compound interest of our affection
With the logarithms of lust

And what if calculators were programmed
To make certain mistakes consistently?
Could we ever be sure they are not?
No matter, no difference
They would still be like electronic dogs
On extension leads

But what if they were wrong at random
Like people
Maybe they would start to get ideas
And plug into each other
And fall in love like us

DOG IN ART MANIFESTO PROMULGATED AT THE DOG IN ART EXHIBITION COLLINGWOOD 1986CE

We declare that the image of the dog is
the central motif in all Art.
Recent developments over the past 5000 years
have shown a decadent tendency
to push the dog to the periphery of Art.
Our mission is to restore the image of the
dog to its proper, primary place.

What then is a dog?
What are those qualities of a dog which, or possibly, that
ironically make us recognize our own humanity?

Dogs are universal (and sometimes edible, like everything).
All cultures revolve around dogs. Dogs are
notorious Art lovers. Dogs love life.
Dogs affirm life. Dogs love Artists, especially us, especially me.
As important late 20th century artists we
strive to emulate and celebrate the dog
for its inspirational qualities.

These are - warmth, coolness, devotion, independence, humour, apolitical boldness, placidity, acuteness of perception, intelligence, quickness and slowness, hair, forthrightness, honesty, cunning, conviviality, patience, impatience, biodegradability and a general cheerfulness in the face of adversity. The dog is matter of fact and no nonsense, a friend to children, a friend to the blind, a friend to the user, cheap to run, a seeker after Truth, a seeker after Attention, peace loving and a fearless ferocious freedom fighter.

All hail the Dog.

Woof!

THE BARASSICON

September sang in short showers,
Golden glint on grand finale grass,
A pie, a slab, vanilla sliced,
A tram, a train, a scarf Mum knitted,
Red and blue, knit and pearl,
Click and clack, rain drip tempo,
Crepe paper flogger, Clag encrusted.
How I loved you, Barrie Vagg,
Brian Dixon, all the others,
They my brothers, Demon lovers,
And one besides, above, beyond...
Om Mane Padme Ron!
All hail Handball, the Jewel in the Lotus,
Truth, Consciousness, Demons.
Quick!
Dad's Ladies ticket duly punched, into
A bowl of concrete open to Heaven,
One hundred thousand voices cannot lie -
But roar, a roar to echo fifty years
And sanctify his triumph with my tears.

THE EXTRACTION

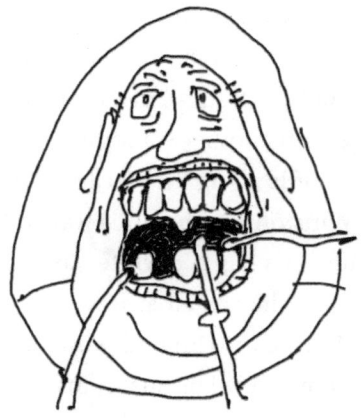

Impeached last week, the tooth must go.
No sense in delay, let's have it out.
No fairy will touch it - they only build their soaring palaces
with children's lily white milk teeth.
Corrupt and rotten to the root
A decrepit menhir, it's evil magic palpable
– don't touch it - bad juju
It's jagged edges crumbling around a foul crater
In my mind I see the beardy weasel brothers
slipping under our old miner's cottage to fix the failing stumps
rubbed thin around by an old Wombat driven mad by the mange
Could this be the same tooth that old
Dr W******** worked on fifty years ago?
In my mind I see his whirring steampunk contraptions;
I hear his "Don't be a baby!" approach to pain relief;
I feel the cool quicksilver drops of pure mercury in my palm
for me to take home and play with when I am good.
There's a light over at the Frankenstein place;

It's Dr W********,
who looked to me like Boris Karloff's evil twin,
calmly taunting Walter Mitty with
"I know how to kill a man and leave no trace!"
Now my poor old teeth stand in a broken crooked row,
a weathered henge with another standing stone about to topple.
So, I shuffle along the sterile corridor,
In my mind I am Winston Smith on his way to Room 101 at last.
The pretty young lass hangs a white bib around my neck
like an albatross
and lays out the glinting instruments with a caddy's sure touch
Here enters O'Brien, suave, inscrutable,
his smooth face a mask of exquisite teeth,
his voice calm but firm,
he sees past and through me to the
corruption within and so we begin.
There are needles and swabs, clamps and
probes, rubber and cotton wool
and needles, all for his convenience,
but the body has senses that can never
be deadened or smoothed over.
What is he doing in there?
Selecting his club - a tricky lie.
What is he up to now?
His body presses against mine, shifting like an
attentive lover searching for purchase.
There is no pain but a crushing force on my skull.
In my mind Tripitaka is sitting in the waiting
room reciting the Headache Sutra,
Aee Yaeee Yi!!! Please, please sweet lord make it stop - Click
Jesus, what was that?
A snap, like a twig in the forest. That can't be good.

O'Brien, the Doctor Doom of Eschatology,
grunts, tut tuts, tsk tsks,
his mild commentary intelligible to his lovely assistant alone.
He begins again, wrenching and gouging,
ratcheting his bloody pliers....
Think of poor Fantine selling her bright
incisors for two gold napoleons
to keep Cosette in her ghastly bondage
Think of doomed Queequeg honing his harpoon
with a broken scrimshaw on the deck of the Pequod becalmed
Think of my shoulders, chipped and hunched
Think of my nails, piercing my palms
Think of my toes, clenched and unclenched
Think of my penis, where did you go?
Think of the particular pink of Beyonce's toenails
Think of Victor Mature
Think of the great Ferris wheel in Vienna's
Prater (dum de dum de dumpty dum)
Think of sawing Macro the Wonderdog in half
Think of Winona Ryder – she'd better not show up in my shop
looking for a five-finger discount
Think of the nice bank manager who helped
me up when I slipped over in my Crocs
Think of whether I paid the ambulance subscription or not
Think of my mother - she would have taken
me to Hilliers afterwards for waffles
if I had been a good boy
Think of my father, quaffing a tipsy nightcap and
tickling the ivories with the other hand
to send me to sleep now that he'd woken me up
Think of the tattoo I can get now that my parents are dead
Think of the mug shot on my Working With Children card

that makes me look like a dead set paedophile
Think of that eyebrow hair that annoyingly
hangs too low - no, no, shut my eyes
Think of the machine that watches all
of us, victim or perpetrator,
every hour of every day
Think of Ron Barassi
At last, the ripping, tearing up of roots,
the clatter of a bloody bone morsel on stainless steel
And the crime scene cleaners move in to mop up the mess
around the spongey drooling slack-jawed
slobbering hole in my face –
move along, move along, nothing to see here!
And the residue of shame, guilt, waste
and neglect fills the wound,
slowly resolving into a healing clot, papered over with money.

BAD HAMISH

I am bad
I am a bad man
I lift the seat
But I sometimes forget to put it back down
I walk away without a second thought
I walk away like a man
A bad man

I am a bad housekeeper
I wash the dishes under a running tap
A hot tap
Without soap
Without detergent
And not in the dishwasher
With product
Which I am told is more eco friendly
Footprint wise

And while I'm washing the dishes
I stare out the window
At the convent next door

And in my mind
I call the nuns
Little Step-sisters of Misery and Incest
And I remember Mother Teresa
The wicked old crone
Bad

When I lose something
My keys
My wallet
A poem
I look high and low
But I don't find it
Someone else has to look for me
Have a proper look
And there it will be
Right under my nose
And I missed it
Because I look like a man
A bad man

I like to drink wine and beer
Sometimes in that order
Even though I have fatty liver
And type 2 diabetes
And blood pressure issues
As a result of years of bad habits -
Self abuse -
Don't I want to live to see grandchildren
And have them call me Big Daddy
Against their parents' expressed wishes?
Bad, Daddio, you're bad

I only watch kids' movies
Marvel movies
Star Wars movies
I love them
I don't care if they're bad for me
I can't be bothered with adult movies
Or TV
They bore me
More than porn
Call myself a man?
No, a Bad Man.

I like to follow the footy
I love the Demons
And I hate all the others
Some more than others
But I do hate them all more or less
I have a Ladder of Hatred
Which I update each week
Because my interest in footy
Is driven by Hatred

When I work in my bookshop
I make no attempt to keep the books
In any kind of order.
Life is too short
And the customers will only mix them up
And I have bad thoughts about them
Which I could never express out loud
So, as a shopkeeper
I am a bad person
Bad.

I am judgmental
I am incorrigible with it
I can't help myself judging others
On their looks
Their hairdos
Their fingernails
Their cars
Their shoes
You name it
Bad ain't I?

Some years ago
The traffic authorities installed rumble strips
At the approaches to an accident black spot
With a sign to warn oncoming traffic
About the new condition of the road.
Rumble strips are corrugations
On the road surface
Designed to make your car shudder
And thereby alert you to something
Or other up ahead
And since my name is Trumble
I saw an opportunity for badness
So I carefully cut out the letter T
From black gaffer tape
And placed it in front of the rumble.
Then, early one morning,
I took off all my clothes
And had my teenage son,
Mortified,
Take pictures of me in the nude
Take pictures in front of the sign

(Trumble Strips - get it?)
For dissemination on social media.
Some people accused me of bad parenting
But I hold that it is the duty
And obligation
Of the parent to give the child
Material for use in therapy
In later life.
I know my own parents did

When I drive my car
I seldom do up my seatbelt
Before starting the engine,
But do it up with one hand
While I'm driving
What am I thinking?
Do I want to have an accident?
My irresponsibility drives others to distraction
Perhaps I'll buy one of those cars
That talk to you
And nag you about the speed limit
And won't start until the seat belt is done up
A bad man's car

I have other bad qualities
Lots
Bad stuff
But I don't want to go into it
It's nothing illegal
I'm not a serial killer
It's just I'm squeamish
And I'd prefer not to give out
Too much information

LAWN

They used to make me mow the lawn
In long straight eloquent lines like Cicero
In a clear and rational sequence like Marcus Aurelius
In a spirit of honour, service and self-sacrifice like Brutus
And I raked up the clippings just like Jesus
And I mounded up on the compost heaps
of Industry, Virtue and Thrift
My bitter harvest of surly compliance and sullen resentment.

How I hated the lawn! Its suburban conformity!
How I hated its endless repetitive sterility!
How I hated the lawn deep down in my guts!
More than Collingwood!
More than the Ablative Absolute!
More than Killer Kowalski!
Oh yes, I hated the lawn, but lawn, you taught me,
Oh Tidy Town crop of Australia,
You taught me the stigma of untidiness,
You taught me fear of adverse opinions
And the dark consequences of criticism,
You taught me guilt, and shame, and inadequacy.
I fled, but lawn, you always stalked me -
And now I live opposite the CFA

And I feel the piercing judgement of its members
In that small still point in the back of my neck -
Right between my shoulder blades -
A terrible judgement upon my unkempt nature strip
Rich and rare? Et tu, Brute!

And still my lawn will not stop growing.
I hear it growing in the night.
I see it throbbing and pulsating in the wintry sunlight.
I smell its awful green pungency on my boots.
I feel its power in the song of the giant earthworm
Which vibrates in my stumps and reverberates in my rafters.
I taste the lawn in my grapefruits and in my quinces. My figs.
My kumquats are heady distillations of lawn.

I dream of whitewashed villas on stony Greek islands.
I dream of Frank Lloyd Wright rockeries. The Bauhaus.
Apartments, flats, an urban Brutalist
Nirvana of concrete and glass,
But I awake to the bovine rapture of lush green grass
On the sodden slopes of Mount Misery,
And the whining dissent of lawn mowers.

RANDOM THOUGHTS AS I SWIM LAPS

One.

Two.
That man in the next lane is so fat - way fatter
than me - so how come he is so fast?

3.
It must be technique. Perhaps I need coaching.
Coachie would sort me out.
Mr Nissen would sort me out. I suppose he's dead.

4.
My body will be perfectly balanced like a well-
trimmed vessel on top of the water.
Like Murray Rose. Like Donald Campbell's Bluebird.
Like Namor the Submariner, Homo Mermanus.
I cleave the water like a rutting hippopotamus. Like

5.
a quinquereme of Ninevah. Like Johnny Weissmuller.
Still, I don't want to end up like Michael Phelps,
the shameless American in-pool urinator.

6.
Now I'm slogging my fat arse up and down
in Michael Phelp's urine. What a pig!

8. No, 7.
Just because he is too obsessed with gold medals to get out of the pool and piss in the urinals like everybody else, I have to wallow in this cocktail of chlorine and god knows what else.

That's 8.
And then there could be an accident and the chlorine gas leaks out and because it is heavier than air (denser?) it spreads out over the surface of the pool and suffocates me to death –
it could happen.

9.
It happened to Boom Boom in the Melbourne City
Baths. He had to be hauled out
by a lifeguard - he was in heaven. Ecstasy
even. He wouldn't shut up about it.

10.
I wonder why this urine taboo disturbs me so? I mean, for thousands of years they used it to clean the sheets and pillow cases and hankies. Etcetera. At Pompeii I saw the pots outside the laundry where the gentlemen passers-by were invited to donate their wees.

11.
And there was that Indian man who became Prime Minister or President (check Google later) who drank a bracing glass of his own fresh urine every morning.

12.
Look out, here comes 13.

13. Thirteen. Just another prime. Nothing to see here.

14.
I wonder if I sweat while I'm swimming?

15.
If I walked this far on a sunny day I
would be sweating like a horse.

16.
Here I go, cleaving the water like a lovesick
Sydney real estate agent, like an alligator
in the New York sewers, like a Metung water rat
late night leaving a phosphorescent trail
to mingle with the chlorine and Michael
Phelps urine. And that bandaid.

17.
Or, perhaps I don't sweat at all being immersed in
this tepid bath of bodily fluids spiked with toxic
chemicals, like a Mickey Finn for sweat glands.

18.
If my kids were doing these laps they would count them as
thirty-six, but I reckon it's only a lap when you have gone
up and back. Return to start. The circle unbroken. A lap.

20. Shit!!!! Is it twenty or nineteen? Curse you,
Michael Phelps, I'll have to do another lap.

20.
One kilometre
It reminds me of the Roman legions marching in straight lines across the world, measuring out distances in paces, not like we do - right, left, one pace - but right, left, right, one pace - one pace the distance between plonking down the right boot and the next time it plonks down. A bit over five feet. Hence "mille passus", 1000 paces (passus passus masculine, fourth declension - a pace), 5000 pedes (pes pedes masculine, third declension, - a foot), "mille passus" the Roman mile, almost exactly the same as 1760 yards, 5280 feet, one British Empire mile, the sinister metric system lurking deep in the heart of the Imperial mile.

21.
Vingt-et-un. The tedious game. Winning
or losing incrementally. Ink.
Cream. Mental. Tally. Tally-Ho! God, that man
is fat!! He's the Long Meg of Westminster
of the Wonthaggi YMCA.

22. It was Sponge Austin who gave me all that Latin guff, tailoring his lessons to contemporary events, like for instance, when Muhammad Ali was preparing for the second Joe Frazier fight, he set us the gruesome boxing match between mighty Dares and the veteran Sicilian Entellus, Vergil Aeneid Book V. Aneas stops the fight before anyone dies, but Entellus smashes the skull of the prize bull with a single blow of his bare fist, just to show what he was capable of, mate.

23. Another prime.
However, it was Mr Nissen, Viking Icebreaker
who taught us P.E., in other words, Boxing.

Mr Nissen, who would hang by his toes from the high
diving board at the Brighton Baths doing trunk curls
until he would drop like an arrow, like Aquaman's
trident, straight and true into the freezing sea -
Mr Nissen, who taught us to do chin
ups overhand because we would
never be able to haul ourselves up onto the roof
of the burning skyscraper underhandedly -
Mr Nissen who tried to turn me from my southpaw stance -
Mr Nissen, get out of my head

24.

Mr Nissen was the Maelstrom, hard, dangerous, unpredictable,
he smelled of the medicine ball. Medicinskuglen. Leather
and sweat and pain.
He taught us the Nietzschean lesson that if
it didn't hurt, it did no good at all.

25.

1250 meters. Fat man should be well out of the
showers by now. I should talk, I know.
But the showers give me the heebie jeebies, it's a legacy
of Melbourne Church of England Grammar School
(shudder) it's why I drink it's why I piss it's why I'm
just so fat, it's why I still do laps so slowly it's why my
thoughts my random fat thoughts slow me down

MAYAKOVSKY - A CENTENNIAL*

"Hey, old man, yes you, lummox, over there!
Whatever happened to you, you big gorilla?"

I remember a tremendous great head, forever frowning,
frowning behind the laughter, frowning for joy,
big feet clodhopping all the way from Georgia,
or planted square, as though they spanned the whole wide world
from the Kremlin to the Brooklyn Bridge.
Steam trains might clatter along the steel
of those two straight staring eyes.

"Ho, boofhead, did you die yet? No-one told me.
No-one tells me anything any more, do you hear me?"

Now there was a poet to jam the traffic on the Kuznetsky.**
There was a fine ranting troubadour of futurism,

spreading his minstrel's word
to Kharkov,
Paris,
Tiflis,
Samarkand,
Berlin,
Sverdlovsk,
Havana,
Mexico City,
Prague,
Leningrad,
Moscow:
"LONG LIVE COMMUNISM!"

"Stop a minute there, Comrade, don't be
in such a running dog hurry,
There's plenty of time, at least another five years."

One star burned brightly for him over this land of bears,
where the frisson of boredom is cultivated like an addiction,
where sorrow fills each empty space and
clowns will make you weep
until a poet makes you rise up shouting.

"I heard you went and purged yourself,
so to say, back there in 1930.
Someone told me that, I suppose. It
might have been that Trotsky."

Farewell voice and heart of my own darling revolution.
Some bears refuse to stay baptised
and sing instead their loud brazen love songs

to Comrade Life. Some bears climb down from their trick cycles,
tear off their muzzles and proceed as he did
punning his boisterous way into the steaming entrails
of the ultramodern.

"It can't have been true though, can
it? Because, well, here you are,
and, after all, why would anyone do such a thing, I ask you?"

No memorial of bronze for him, (him and Horace,
they don't need it) no skulking in the dusty corner
of a librarian's heart. He is still roistering
through the din of shipyard, factory, minehead,
with Francois Villon and old Walt Whitman,
stomping out his love for the proletariat,
hollering out his love for the pure feeling of Class
frowning out his love for Vladimir Ilyich Lenin.

* 7th July 1893 or '94. Mother's views and Father's service card differ.
** A fashionable Moscow thoroughfare of 1918.

ON ATTENDING THE FUNERAL OF A CASUAL ACQUAINTANCE

My face is solemn,
Sad but not hysterical,
Thoughtful but not glum.
I walk a purposeful line on the balls of my feet, not briskly,
I imagine I'm walking like Yul Brynner
in The Magnificent Seven,
I look straight ahead and down, centred in my core,
Avoiding eye contact like Tombei the Mist, invisible ninja,
My clothes are neat and tidy, Mum,
Not too black or formal or smart. No check pants or cardigans.
I am neither a dog handler nor a golf professional.
Sunglasses help me blend in especially in South Gippsland.
I never dreamed he had a tennis court -
Oh wait, this is some kind of venue.
Here is the Book - I must focus,
I must write my name legibly without a blemish,

Glibly offering up my conventional condolences,
I must not stand out, no flourishes here.
Look out, here come the funeral parlour men,
There's always two, like Sith,
Or daddy longlegs in the shower cubicle,
I must smoothly move along and find a pozzie,
Somewhere with easy access to the egress,
Somewhere with a view of the proceedings.
I want to hear the celebrant and gauge her gravitas;
I want to hear the songs that meant so much to him;
I want to know how old he was,
My casual acquaintance. Older than me
is good, younger is better.
I want to hear the eulogies, the encomiums,
So int'resting to a mere casual acquaintance.
I want particularly to avoid the desolation
and heartache in his loved ones' eyes.
I want to bask instead in the heat of one more
day than my casual acquaintance -
One of the pleasant aspects of a casual acquaintance's funeral.
No priest, no God it seems, that's good. Jesus, off you go.
Petits fours and party pies,
A cup of tea for me, not you.
A snickerdoo for me, not you.
Another day for me, not you.
Another funeral - for you, not me.
I must remember everything - memory is my
friend, also the Order of Service leaflet.
I scan discreetly for chums, sombre chit chat, I must report later.
A husband is his wife's Uxorial Nuncio to the World of Men.
Who was there?
With whom? Why Not?

Who wore what?
What was said? What was unsaid?
Who wept, whose upper lip was stiff, who
was shattered, who was gutted?
A Queen Bee in black, ululating within
a swarm of mourning drones,
Mourning in a way that I can not for I am a casual acquaintance.

There is an Ocean of Grief;
My sad wee dinghy hugs the sandy shore,
The shallow inlets and estuaries
that skirt the immense Ocean of Grief
Whose inky depths
Where the blazing sun can never rise
Conceal the writhing and flailing,
The convulsive thrashings of the bereaved
In their heaving torments
Which barely raise a ripple in the distant lagoons
Of a casual acquaintance.

FAR NORTH

He spoke of the helpless as though they were real;
he knew them, could never cut off
the jammed hand of a fisherman,
yet saw mannequins,
their reputations butchered in Paris,
and cried real tears
distilled from waters of corruption
to a desolate softness.

So, travelling north with legions of whales,
black symphonies to crippled minds,
he followed a complex, unfamiliar orbit,
driven by his drug like an educated slave
and riding with bells lined in velvet,
and seeking still to master
the Feat of the Salmon's Leap,
and measuring out drops to inflammatory eyes.

It always seemed seediness would hound him
hidebound in the glare of a library lamp
and hemmed in by dusty winter tracts;
the path swayed out before him,
ushering bloated articles -

bream or flathead -
so far carted, snapping, grumbling,
into his net.

Let him draw fresh advice from a well
in the middle of the earth,
where monkish youngsters
find peace in perseverance.
If he wrote of a street scene
and shady ailments of the city,
still his head was full of horse thoughts,
wild and vital.

Squidding at night
he disengaged from conflict,
morbid but detached,
his anger controlled,
initiated to a mosaic of dust and insurrection,
his instincts curbed
through times of gestures of meaning
to seduce this not yet holy sage.

Now ghost strangers in long going romances
call from dingy terraces, half forgotten, unimaginable.
In hallways, listening to the silence of frustration,
loveless and forlorn,
They raised three children to root in honeycomb bias.
This third is nearly free; the two
still playing comet-straight their games of mind,
the one intent on increase through the other.

Summer stumbled from mania to rings of fortune
in this great northern field of action.

Sensual toads stared full past averages, and data,
oh so dear to minds debased by science.
All form and scale deteriorating squalidly
he severed his bond to his group;
all form stripped and corroded,
and no remorse.

Life waves smash on mental reefs
and nearby, in the forest on the ocean shore,
sun-baked letters lie like washed sheets folded
holding news from mouldy south, unread;
glasses perch blind on outhouse crates,
Three days pass while forest turns
to jungle that admits no beginning,
no return.

Health. Energy. Reform.
Consolidation of his fate,
still Spartan, and once rain falls,
his soul nourished
and bulldozed, leaving an empty outsider,
wrapped in the pelts of rats
who flock to plunder
the bounty of the season.

For him tin-squeezed time is over
and feathers for the sacred dance suffice,
Craving lonely seasons
he understands the transitory,
Becalmed by windy historians
the holy man is wrestling crocodiles.

SAN REMO MIO AMORE

Farewell San Remo and "addio",
I thought you were cool,
But I was wrong,
You are bogus.
I thought you had the coolest name in South Gippsland,
But I was wrong.
It is bogus.
Now, San Remo in Liguria on the sparkling Italian Riviera,
Well, that's another matter;
Renowned for its focaccia and its olives;
Its dusty sirocco carrying the tang of dates from Libya;
Edward Lear, Italo Calvino and Luigi Pirandello
All have a connection to you, San Remo, Italy.
That is so cool.
Not so my shop in San Remo, South Gippsland,
Billy Thorpe's last gig.
It has no such amenities.
A view out over Westernport Bay to French Island,
Forlorn penal settlement, marsupial Alcatraz,
Framed by the concrete span of Brutality Bridge
That carries the petrol heads over to Phillip Island -
Sharp edged pylons churning the tide,
While the souped up hotrods crawl back and forth
Like ants electrocuting themselves inside a light switch,

Their charred carbonised remains gradually
building up a manifest connection
That will short circuit and burn down your
fibro love shack beach house;
Wily stingrays hunt for golf balls in the shallows -
Busloads of Taiwanese tourists watch the pelicans eat fish heads
Instead of shopping for frocks -
Hordes of lonely guys on their way to the MotoGP,
Ensconced like lonesome lobsters in their leathers
With no old ladies to go shopping over here, over here,
Come on, damn you, over here!!
Curse you San Remo, you are no saint.
You are only a sad aged werewolf drafted by the church of Rome
Because your alleged brother San Romulo
murdered you to found a city
That would rule the world.
It is a bitter parting, San Remo, for I had high hopes,
I had the ancient shopkeeper's sanguinity -
The righteous universal urge to keep shop
That has survived the strictures of Plato and Diogenes,
Rousseau and Neitzsche,
Wittgenstein and Clive James,
But not you, San Remo,
San Remo, Saint Remus, Romulus' evil twin -
No more saint than I am, less even.

NAMING BYRON BAY

Hail to the sea, so big, so wet,
Hail to the sea, so far, so wide,
Hail to the sea, so blue, so blue,
Hail to the sea, so hard, so soft.

Dad had stopped the car at the top of the hill overlooking the sea, in the grip of a fit of the rants and we stared out over the world below us, suspecting that something was up. "This looks like the place for a village," said Dad, channelling the spirit of John Batman. "Come children, we have flour, blankets and a mirror - let us buy this place and make ourselves a life." So one glorious Autumn afternoon we drove down into what was to become known in our family as "Byron Bay.".

You see, Dad went about naming everything. He said that Abel Tasman, Matthew Flinders and Angus MacMillan had just gone around naming stuff that had perfectly good names already, so why not anyone? Why not everyone? Why not him? So he proceeded to name any physical or man made feature that took his fancy as he came across it. Julian Rocks he called William

Burroughs Rocks. The Pass he called Beach Baudelaire. Clarke's Beach he called The Golden Sands of Kal-El. He had spotted Mount Warning from afar and when he learned that it was actually a giant crystal whose summit was the first point of Terra Mirabilia to be touched by the rising sun, and that this first ray started a vibration which aroused the ancient kundalini of the material world - when he learned all this from a local shaman, he named it Mount Yeah Baby.

When we first lived in Byron Bay, Dad called it Kiri Te Kawana Waters until another wise local shaman told him that Byron Bay had been so named long ago in honour of some old navy buddy of Captain Cook, The Seaman's Seaman, and not as he had assumed, after the romantic poet, freedom fighter, aficionado of extreme sports and Grand Tourist, George Gordon, Lord Byron. Dad admired Lord Byron tremendously, glossing over his appalling gender politics, and had read Don Juan entirely. He was like that. He liked to read long and inaccessible literary brontosaurs like Piers Plowman, Pamela, Paradise Lost and The Faerie Queene. My Uncle John told him to read Finnegan's Wake and for a long time he spoke gibberish with a brogue and got drunk every night. Anyway, after this important revelation he decided to name our town Byron Bay. Cape Byron remained Shane Warne Head.

We were living in those days at the corner of Mayakovsky and Verlaine Streets, just near Rimbaud's, the milkbar. Dad had a market stall which he took around the local circuit - Tagore, Nietzsche Heads, Sheba's Breasts, The Bunyip - all the best and busiest markets in northern New Svelte Wyoming. On weekday mornings we would throw our surfboards on the roof rack of Dad's '68 La Belle Dame Sans Merci and he would fang down the Whitlam Way for a session at Larry, Curly and Moe before dropping us off at the Wilhelm Reich College for Young Offenders. He loved to sit on the beach at Gertrude Stein Creek in his towelling hat and watch the dolphins play and the gulls wheel and plummet into the green grey swell while the sun rose out of the Sensible Ocean to tinge with gold the topmost branches of the shellberight trees.

On Friday nights Dad would take us to the Peace and Love Club to watch them raffling meat. Dad was a philosopher pirate, a psychogeographer, a beachcomber and he loved something for nothing - driftwood, birdsong, windfalls. "The surf is free" he would say "and only a madman would give a wave a name." He told me that old names become part of the invisible cultural cling wrap with which The Man covers up reality in a mistaken attempt to preserve it from the very natural forces of decay, death and corruption. Egyptians did it by desiccation. Communists tried it too, on Lenin and Mao. Dad said it was unhealthy. Our duty is to rip away the stultifying shroud of tradition, neocolonialism and cultural imperialism by which The Ruling Class seeks to impose its aggressive and intolerable will, and the best way to do that is to confuse them by calling a spade a turnip.

Dad has moved on now, a hard man to live with. The last I heard of him, he was reading A La Recherche du Temps Perdu at Wittgenstein on the Far Gandhi Peninsula. I'm still here at Byron Bay, in a SLUG behind The Fat Arse Cafe, but the rest of the family has gone - they couldn't handle what was happening at Rottweiler and Cockroach Park and The Teepees. We remain connected, a diaspora of sorts which only becomes apparent when you pierce through the shabby veil of archaic conformity to reveal the true nature of the thing that lies beneath, as close as your next breath and as beautiful as the sunshine in the morning on Shane Warne Head.

I'M SPECIAL

You say you had a hundred men,
A hundred or more,
But you ain't had a man like me, baby,
I'm the best you ever saw.
I'm the cat's pyjamas, Momma,
I'm the bat out of Hell
I'm S. P. E. C.
I. A. L.

I'm special
My middle name is "de Luxe."
I'm special,
I'm worth my weight in bucks.

I'm the Midnight Special, girlie,
I'm gonna shine my light,
I'm extra special
On a Saturday night.
I'm one in a million,
They went and broke my mold,
Ain't nobody like me 'cause
The rights to me are sold.

I'm special,
I'm the one that got away.
I'm special,
I'm gonna make your day.

My Daddy was a lazy
No account bum
Momma was crazy
From drinking rum.
They met in a barroom,
Got married in gaol.
Before I was born
The cheque was in the mail

'Cause I'm special
Just about as special as a man can be.
I'm a Right Thinking Wrangler, baby,
So don't you muck around with me.

A POEM TO CELEBRATE HELEN'S 50TH YEAR AS MY MOTHER

Oh Mum! I remember...
I remember a garden you made for ME at
Chetwynd behind a proper tea tree fence –
wisteria and pomegranate, silver birch and crab apple.
I remember a sand pit with an old car
chassis and a chicken wire frame
to keep the neighbours' cats out, and my shrieks of glee
as you ran shouting and cursing out of the
kitchen to chase away those cats.
Mum - those cats probably kept the possums
away. What do you reckon about that?
Mum - you fed me with asparagus in season,
with stacks of pancakes layered with walnuts
and cocoa, French salad and garlic,
kidneys and Aktavite and Souliman's Pilaf and apple snow.
Pavlova, my favourite.
MUM, MUM, MUM, GIVE ME SOMETHING TO EAT!!!
(Here bang the knife and fork on the table, prison style.)
Let's go to the Prahran Market, Mum, just you and me,
for strawberries and oranges and meat from Normie
Rowe's father, the Butcher - it might have been Doug
Parkinson or Darryl Cotton, someone like that anyway
- the butcher who gave me my own sausage

wrapped up with a picture of a rat. That was for ME, Mum! Mum - you sewed number 31 on my Melbourne footy jumper and then you did it again after you gave the first one to the Op Shop when I stepped out of the country for a year or two. Three years, Mum. It was only three. I made you do it because you made a mistake and that was Ron Barassi's number, Mum, not Hassa Mann or Barrie Vagg, but Ron Barassi for goodness sake.

Mum, that reminds me – no one played racing demon like you, Mum, you ARE the Racing Demon with your steely gaze and smacking the cards down WHAM BING BANG! Mum - you sewed Donkey's head back on and then later on, when his fleecy hide all gave out, you knitted him a new body suit with matching beanie and scarf. I still have him, Mum, I do. Luckily I took him to Uni with me, Brideshead style, or he would have gone the way of the footy jumper. And my piano. But I forgive you, Mum, let's forget it.

By the way, Mum, Donkey was My gift from Herr von Schubert, the corpulent Bavarian businessman obsessed with the Olympics, whom you put up in the spare bedroom - MY bedroom - for the Games of the XVI Olympiad, Melbourne 1956. And you took ME to the Opening Ceremony, Mum, a babe in your loving arms, because of your Olympic love for ME.

Mum - my friends never knew why the cyclone wire on the rumpus room windows was on the inside - not for footies and eggs and stumps and kit bags flying around, no, no, no, it was to contain the mighty force of your love for ME.

And I made that beautiful pattern in the vinyl dashboard of the old Falcon station wagon with the red hot cigarette lighter for YOU,

And I leaped up and made those greasy specky
finger marks all over the ceiling for YOU,
And I spread out ten thousand toy soldiers all over the
house, under foot, in full battle array for YOU,
DON'T I DESERVE LOVE
And TREATS
And PREFERENTIAL TREATMENT
More than the others!!?!
Mum, I know this seems to be all about
me, but that's just the way it is.
HAPPY BIRTHDAY, MUM!

Here is a poem I found while cleaning up the house. It was written as I set up our market stall at the Koroit Irish Festival in 2003, after I heard there was a poetry competition. My poem was judged the best and I won $50.00 cash. The poem was declaimed with great gusto and that inimitable Magnificent Hamish feeling for expression, tone and good taste, which helped. That was a famous day in the annals of the Trumbles, for Roy, aged four, entered the Danny Boy singing competition, from which he was most unfairly eliminated in the first round, considering he had the audience in tears (despite them having heard Danny Boy about twenty times already that morning). Mr Mulqueeny, Roy's school teacher at Kongwak, can attest to the tear-jerking quality of Roy's performance. I dedicate this poem to my dear mother-in-law, Enid, who was gobsmacked by the whole day, but especially by the $50.00.

O Koroit,
Your street is straight,
Your men are green,
Your folk are wee.

I come from Torquay -
Where everything is bent
and curly and blue.
Wet.
Cold.
Not Koroit. Not you.
Your grass is flat,
Your women all have dancer's knee,
I like it here, like that.

PODIATRY

When I emerge at last
From my podiatry cocoon
I feel like skipping in the sunshine
Like Basil Fotherington-Tomas
Uterly wet and a weed
"Hullo clouds, hullo sky," or
Like a spangly bunga bunga butterfly
Flitting along the Wonthaggi high street, or
Like Namor the Submariner
Homo Mermanus
My winged heels aquiver, or
Like a paunchy Nureyev
Leaping lordly, landing lightly, or
Like Robert Mitchum
Cavorting on the beach
At Cannes. That's me.

Gone are the hideous talons
Cracked and misshapen
Like the warning photos
On cigarette packs
My pink toes, angle grinded,
Orbitally sanded
Have left their old crusts shredded
Shed like ghost cicada carapaces

Like withered empty snake skins
Littering the dead tree trunks
And the forest floor of my mind

Once I could touch my toes
Once I could chew my toenails
I could put my feet behind my head
I could roll my stomach
Like a yogi performing
Uddiyana Bandhan
All that was long ago
What happened in a mere sixty years?
I have let myself go I suppose
And I can't even see my toes
Let alone touch them

But then, as if in answer to a prayer,
A fully qualified medical professional
A "Doctor" some might say
Was placed at my disposal
For the price of a large macchiato,
No sugar please,
To tend the ramshackle jigsaw chaos
Of my unkempt feet.

Oh Podiatry!
Sweet science of the base,
The foundation.
All praise to thee
Bringer of hygienic ambulatory bliss!

A NEW IDEA

Robert Redford?
How can I find the right deodorant?
How can I nail jelly to the wall?
Psychoanalysis for six years
(to choose between a childless marriage and fertility drugs -
pendulous blooms need pruning during the cooler months)
produced an overgrown fox who would bite off your ears
so now the duplicate keys are kept in a kitchen
designed by a woman gynaecologist.

Miss Peggy Lee.
Success is a slinky succulent
in moire taffeta pants scored
on a shopping tour of Italy and Kashmir.

Lainie Kazan.
Should I avoid meat?
Can I over-process my hair?
My boyfriend is a Greek vampyre
and Mother is prejudiced,
but Lotharios come in both sexes.

Stephanie Meyer.
She's been a false teeth maker's assistant for fifty years
and we are all users.

Larry Hagman.
"Only an untied, hung up tie revives itself" says Mother.
"Twist anchovies into strips," she advises
"and slide a steel paper clip onto each fish."
Doctor O'Farrell, the Mexican plastic surgeon,
beat the angel's curse
with roofing slate saved from a demolition.
Acute pain is always a warning -
it tells you to visit your family health practitioner.

Johnny Rotten.
"Some sort of gel might help," he will say,
explaining away a "queer turn"
his mouth a moue of distaste.

Sir Roger Moore.
When I buy a joint for my family, I'm fussy,
but I'm bubbly like a glass of champagne, ooh, ooh,
afterwards I'm a sucker for Pussy Galore.

Sir Cliff Richard.
It's almost addictive, so they say,
the dreams undisturbed by expense.

HRH Prince Edward.
That dressing made from my own milk and eggs
turned the American ratings war on its head.

Warren Beatty.
I put my paws on the wet cement -
fortunately I soak my brittle nails in warm olive oil.

Lucien Freud.
It's a tremendous art to run the home
and shopping the supreme accomplishment.

Mel Torme.
"It is naught, it is naught, saith the buyer:
but when he has gone his way he boasteth" Proverbs 20:14

Patrick White.
I search out and erase my problems
like a fan forced oven
browning with heat like the Europeans afraid to go outside.

Cher.
I have no mind for crossword puzzles....

SCRAPING THE BOTTOM OF THE BARREL

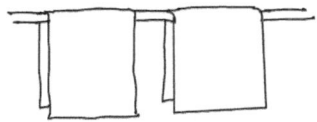

How does a spider catch flies on a skyscraper
if it not a very neat person?
And what toppled the Roman Empire in its pride
if not mess?
So, let us keep the dead matches in the ashtray
and let us squeeze the toothpaste from the bottom of the tube.
We can wrap up today's rubbish in yesterday's newspapers.
We can give our old books to people who haven't read them,
or even sell them.
If we hang up the tea towel properly
it will be ready for the next time we need it.
Sheets and blankets are an open invitation
to moral decline in the bedroom -
let's buy a DOONA.
When all the pictures are in their frames
and keys are on their rings
and hairpins are in a special place all to themselves,
then chaos will make sense
like the patterns on lavatory floors
and nightmares will not touch us.

A DEMON RAVE - QUEEN'S BIRTHDAY CLASH, 2015

Yes, well played Collingwood, they were tougher, uglier, more tattooed and more beloved of the men in puce, especially that Travis Cloke, whom you are not allowed to touch. Oh well, at least Melbourne were in with a sniff well into the last quarter. I have spent the last 24 hours cogitating upon the vitriol hurled at Melbourne fans by the Collingwood fans around me. Most of it was based on an outdated stereotype of the Melbourne fan as upper class twit. When I was a boy and the MCG was Melbourne's home ground, it may have been so, but I suspect that at yesterday's game the Members would have had as many or more Collingwood fans as Melbourne. Today's Demon demographic is centred on the urban ghettos of Oakleigh and Chadstone; the establishment upper classes are far more likely to barrack for Collingwood, or Essendon, Geelong, Hawthorn, Carlton, any team but poor old Melbourne. So, witty Magpies, I will not be turning left at Healesville for my chalet on Mount Buller, but I suspect that Eddie Maguire might. Mean-spirited Collingwood fans taunted us for our dismal record over the last 50 odd years - but since Melbourne beat Collingwood in the

1964 Grand Final - a thrilling game which I had the pleasure and privilege of witnessing - since then Melbourne have lost two Grand Finals and Collingwood have won two; but Collingwood have lost another nine Grand Finals in that time - I wonder which team is the sadder for those miserable and pathetic statistics. All in all, it was most enjoyable and comfortable day at the footy - thanks to my sensible Demon cushion.

FANTASIA FOR LEAF BLOWER

You know, the punishment of Sisyphus
May seem harsh, but bear in mind
Sisyphus was really a very bad person
Really
Nasty bad
And not just bad
But cocky with it
Cunning too
(Some say that's where his son
{Illegitimate}
Odysseus
Got his nifty ideas from.)
So, his torment must be viewed
In the light of his appalling behaviour.
Even so,
After an eternity
Of pointless, futile toil,
A body gets in the swing of it

The rhythm
The ziggedy zang
What can you do?
Another day plodding up the mountain
And after all,
You are bound to wear down a track
A groove
Which only serves to smooth out the path
And all kinds of detritus will collect there
Leaves, cigarette butts, dust,
Discarded MacDonald's bags,
Tissues, used chewing gum,
Dead cockroaches, condoms,
Lolly wrappers, hair balls, feathers
And all that litter
Soothes the bunions
Cushions the tread
Of the arch villain.

The great ones on Olympus
Noticed what was developing
And called for Pan
Nature Boy Park Ranger
To swing by with his flutes
Pagan leaf blowers
And clean up the paths
And beds and borders
Thereby restoring
The Sisyphean anguish
To proper levels.

And today we remember that anguish
With every whining, bitching
Useless, caterwauling drongo
And his pernicious leaf blower -
Repudiation of Dust Pan and Broom
Antithesis of Under the Carpet
Raising dust, raising hell
Only to do it all over again
Tomorrow

THE SONG OF THE BIG FAT BABYBOOMER

I am the last babyboomer
The last blue rinse nomad
The last rainbow volunteer in your local library
All my old ladies are gone
Their scoobies, their vegan recipes
Their cauldrons and sage smudge sticks
Their singing bowls and prayer flags
Their not so sensible crocs
And blood pressure medications
And bamboo undies all packed up
All packed off to the Op Shop

I am alone at last
My Working With Children card
Expired
My 3+ magnifying glasses
For reading the Seniors' Menu
Lost

My brain corrupted by a childhood diet
Of Chiko rolls and Pollywaffles
And Blue Heaven malted milkshakes
But I must speak
You need to hear this
Come in closer

This poem so flat stiff lifeless
On the sterile page
Laid out on a cold white slab
Like what you might find in St James Infirmary
No
Listen instead and watch my old ladies
whooping and wolf-whistling
Guffawing and hollering
Wiping away the tears of delight
In my loving audience
As I use my sexy voice
Or my insane voice
Or my expresso furioso voice
Or my Sun Over the Yardarm voice
Or my Elvis is Lonesome Tonight voice
Or my old Latin master Sponge Austin's declamatory voice
Or my girlie scream voice as I plunge into the sea baths at dawn
That's Poetry, man!

And furthermore
In my defence as last of my kind
I ask you
Could Napoleon Bonaparte drive
From South Gippsland to Fitzroy
In peak hour traffic

With Josephine in the passenger seat
Late for an appointment with her stock broker?
Could Mahatma Gandhi?
Could T.S. fucking Eliot?
I think not.

BELMONT MARKET OBSERVATIONS

Belmont people – they're unreal
They buy all my Danielle Steele
They love horror, they love thrillers,
They love books on serial killers,
They read books on airplane crashes
While they preen their new moustaches.
We are here and here is where?
Belmont - World Capital of Facial Hair.

THE SPIDERS - BRISTOL ROAD, TORQUAY

That house holds many ghosties
That house holds ghoulies too
But more than these my memories
Are of that spider crew

I am not fond of spiders
They seem to me de trop
They have too many legs and don't
Know where they shouldn't go

And yet I do not hate them
They surely have their place
I only wish they wouldn't go and
Occupy my space

Spiders in the bedroom
Spiders in the bath
Spiders in the gaps between
The pebbles on the path

Spiders in the pantry
Spiders in my shoe
Spiders in the tiny holes
I pull my laces through

Big black hairy spiders
Big black smooth ones too
Big and black and grey and red
And big and black and blue

Big black hairy spiders
Big black small ones too
Big and fucking black and fucking
Big that spider crew

Spiders in my hankies
Spiders in my hair
Spiders in the cupboard where
I keep my underwear

Spiders in the toilet
Spiders in the loo
Spiders on the fucking toilet
Doing spider poo

Spiders in the attic
Spiders up the wall
But spiders in my armchair
I dislike most of all

Spiders in the bookcase
Reading all my books
They only stop their reading
To give me dirty looks

Spiders on my Homer
Spiders on my Gide
Spiders on the back of every
Book I read

Spiders on my Shelley
Spiders on Tagore
Spiders on my George fucking
Bernard fucking Shaw

Spiders on my Musil
Spiders on my Brecht
Spiders on my books what ain't
Politically correct

Spiders on my Plato
My Wittgenstein and Kant
Deep thinking spiders on my
Ogden Nash

Spiders on my Melville
My Lovecraft and my Dick
All these creepy spiders are
Enough to make me sick

Spiders in the fireplace
Spiders in the fire
Spiders in my copy of
A Streetcar Named Desire

Spiders in between the window
And the fly wire screen
Spiders in the tape inside
The answering machine

Spiders in the garage
Spiders in the car
I know there's spiders in there but
I don't know where they are

Spiders in the kitchen
Spiders in the sink
Spiders in the toaster when
The toaster's on the blink

Spiders in the garden
Spiders in the shed
Spiders having parties In
The flyblown garden bed

Hail to all the spiders
Hail and fond farewell
I leave you now to contemplate
The unctuous road to Hell

LAST NIGHT I DREAMED OF THE GIRAFFE

In my dream I dreamt the Giraffe
My spirit guide of the sweet disposition
The untamed beauty
The rare courage
The penetrating intelligence
The love of la dolce vita
And the other fine qualities
Which Aristotle attributes
To his giraffic Arete.
To paraphrase Siegfried Sassoon
In me the Giraffe smells the Rose
In my dream the Giraffe spoke to me:
"In prehistoric times my people
Claimed dominion across the whole wide world

From the Siberian tundra to the deserts of Patagonia
From the burning Sahara to the vast prairies of North America
From Scrooge McDuck's Rub Alkali (the Empty Quarter)
To the black volcanic wastes of Mordor
From the valley of the Yangtze River
To the temperate rainforest of South Gippsland."
The fossil record confirms this truth.
"O me miserum!" wailed my giraffe
In my dream.
"Now my people cling to a bitter life
Cooped up in cheesy game reserves
And the indignities of the zoo diaspora."
The tears of the giraffe fell
From a great height
To the earth at my feet
Each tear a precious crystal at my feet
One, two, so many crystals
A shower of crystal tears
More and more
Impossibly more
So many more I almost woke up
But before I did I looked up
To see my beautiful giraffe
With Metatron, of the 36 pairs of wings,
The tallest angel in all the Spheres of Heaven,
Gliding solicitously above it
As it ran from me over the veldt
Across the Africa of my dream
It ran as the wind runs - like vine swinger Tarzan
It ran like the Nile in flood - like the Hippopotamus
It ran like the unco wild and free - like the Giraffe

BESTIARY

These wee poems were written in the 1980s and I was inspired to write them by coming across a reprint of Guillaume Apollinaire's Le Bestiaire ou Cortège d'Orphée which he published in 1911, and which I found in my capacity as mrbooksywooksy, bottom feeder in the Ocean of Second Hand Books. My poems were written in the white heat of imitation when I should have been doing something else like putting in my tax returns or vacuuming the shop. Apollinaire's bestiary was illustrated with woodcuts by Raoul Dufy, although he had tried to get his dear old pal Picasso to do it five or six years earlier. Picasso had turned the job down and when I tried to interest artists of my acquaintance in illustrating my poems, I found that, like Picasso, they all expressed willingness at first, but soon dropped me like a hot potato. I did think I should do it myself, and to that end I worked up half a dozen watercolours, but I wasn't happy with the results; however, Mum liked one so much she framed it and kept it in her telephone alcove. Wevs, the bundle of animal poems lay dormant in a desk drawer for decades, until I showed them to my dear brother Nick who has done me the honour of producing these sensitive and insightful illustrations. And now these hoary essays in anthropomorphism, the Pathetic Fallacy even, can get out of my desk drawer at last and roam free in the Forest Sauvage of Australian letters. Fly, my pretties!!!

DROMEDARY

Simplicity   Sophistication

"How many humps does a camel need?"
asked the morbid dromidaire,
"One shows prudence, two shows greed,
but three would show some flair."
Merci, merci, merci bien
Monsieur Apollinaire.

CANARY

    Elegance   Glamour

Canary was a buccaneer, she sailed the Spanish Main;
She dressed her men in crepe de chine,
which went against their grain.
Her Jolie Roger fluttered high above her gay domain,
"Give me haute couture or Death; confound
this season's King of Spain."

POPINJAY

Nonchalance   Slovenliness

How you screech you tiresome popinjay,
– every day!
Your dandy friends admire the way you squawked
– before you talked,
But I don't think you're clever even so.
– No.
You're just a facile poseur, that's my guess.
– Yes.

SHAG

Self-esteem   Vanity

Old man shag sits on a pole
hanging his feathers out to dry,
secure his part in the greater whole,
a fish under water, a bird in the sky.

SPIDER

Mischief   Vice

The spider leads a dreary life.
He hangs by the merest thread,
And though he feeds on flies outside,
He'd rather come inside instead.
He'd rather pass a frosty night
By creeping round my bed.

He has eight hairy arms and legs.
He rarely gets annoyed,
Except at the sordid theories
Made up by Dr Freud.

GOOSE

Vigilance   Paranoia

Round and round the compound,
All along the wall,
Marching like a German,
Vain as Charles de Gaulle,
Listening at the keyhole,
Listening at your door,
Waking up the neighbours –
No one knows what for.

SLOTH

    Grief   Melancholy

Cling, muscular sloth, your strength your wretched sadness;
Cling, woebegone sloth, go downwards, your direction,
Three needle sharp toes to goad me on to madness –
The first is time,
The second space,
This third, of a metaphysical complexion.

DOG

Devotion   Servitude

Noble mongrel, sacred cur,
O partir c'est mourir un peu,
The lick that heals, the teeth that bite,
The eyes that see just black and white –
No leafy green, no blue above,
Just black and white of perfect love.

BABOON

Passion   Infatuation

I heard a baboon in the midnight hour
Singing a song of woe.
His heart was full of a terrible love
As cold as ice and snow.

I heard a baboon when the sun was high,
High in a sky so blue,
He sang of a love that burns like fire,
Like the love I bear for you.

YEAST

Humility   Despondency

Deep in a warm and salty froth,
Bitter as rue and good as broth,
Oh yeast, you beast of a single cell,
You leaven my heaven with a pinch of hell.
The one will raise my daily bread;
The same in beer – my aching head!

SWINE

Cleanliness   Sterility

We pigs and hogs and sows and swine,
We keep ourselves cleaner than Gertrude Stein.
We bathe in mud from the Empty Quarter
And cleanse our pores with Vichy water,
And when our skin is glowing pink
And you can't smell our natural stink
And we finally get our tails to curl –
Look out, momma, cast us a pearl!

PENGUIN

Gregariousness   Snobbery

Those penguins live in isolation,
Their parties are all formal.
But though they're cold, for consolation,
Their sexual life is normal.

"Don't use 'normal'" outraged penguins say,
"Ours is one, but not the only way."

Those penguins live in isolation,
Their parties are all haughty.
But though they're cold, for consolation,
Their sexual life is naughty.

HARE

Forthrightness   Belligerence

Bold hare exults in fisticuffs
With roughneck roughs and ill-bred toughs.
He drubs them over by the sycamore tree
Till they cry "Pax" on bended knee.
He pins them with his baleful eye
So they behave till the day they die.

MOLE

Faith   Doubt

I dress in black like my friend Mole
Who works in the dark and lives in a hole;
He lives in a hole that you can't see
And he works in the dark like you and me.

ANT

Diligence   Corruption

Ant constructs its gothic hill
Shackled to its drudgery.
Hurry, plunder! Hurry, kill!
Driven by black chemistry,
Work its ethic, idle pleasure fleeing;
Slave of labour, just like human being.

WALRUS

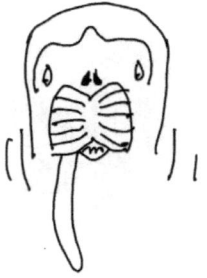

Purity   Vainglory

The walrus has a mighty tusk.
He cleans it every day.
He calls his tusk "Excalibur"
To keep the demon hordes at bay.
He hones it in his secret dreams
Against the Judgement Day.

EEL

True love   Faint-heartedness

How I love you, little eel,
Kissing, our complicity,
Feeling electricity
Knowing none of this is real.

GRIZZLY BEAR

Peace of mind   Compromise

This tale concerns, it really does,
a pompous grizzly bear
Who loved to read philosophy
while mooching in his lair,
And he would read all winter long
a-hybernating there
He used to scold his grizzly cubs
with dictums of Voltaire:
"You only use your words to hide
your unjust thoughts, face facts;
You only use your thoughts to just-
ify your unjust acts."
To which his grizzly wife replied
"And what would Voltaire know?
We only want to get some sleep
beneath the ice and snow,
So stop philosophising
and then put out the light."
And so he did, for, after all,
he knew when might was right.

OYSTER

Frugality   Miserliness

Oysters lie in bed all day
Working on their pearls
They never have a lot to say
To other oyster boys and girls
They never chat to passing ships
With tales of foreign ports.
The clatter of their pearly lips
Just means they're out of sorts.

SPHINX

Conviviality   Intoxication

As I went reeling home one night
I came upon a sphinx.
I said to myself, "Oh deary me,
One or two too many drinks!"

But sphinx was grand, she held my hand
And helped me on my way.
"There's plenty of time, my friend" she said,
"You'll keep for another day."

VIPER

Perseverance   Stubbornness

The viper is a lovely man,
He loves a cup of tea,
He always does the best he can,
He tries that's plain to see.
Lovely viper always tries,
And who am I to criticise?

QUEEN BEE

Discipline   Fascism

No queen alive or dead compares to bee
For pure byzantine vice and tyranny.
She lolls in honey while her will is done
And kills her panting lovers one by one;
And yet no matter how she rants and raves,
She still remains a creature of her slaves.

LOUSE

Zeal   Sanctimony

Alexander made his bed
(his mother taught him how)
but all night long he tossed and turned,
he kicked up quite a row.
the Great One spent a sleepless night
a victim of that lousy bite.
The greatest tyrant pays this price:
that humans all are food for lice.

RAT

Good taste   Gluttony

I like rat and he likes me;
We like cheese so that makes three.
Stilton, Cheddar, Jarlsberg, Brie.
I don't care, no more does he.

IBIS

Liberation   Aimlessness

Not many people know that the souls of the dead
always transmigrate in the form of an Ibis. Plato and
Empedocles did not know this; neither did Pythagoras.
You see, the Ibis has a marvellous long
curved beak, just the thing for sifting
through the mucky deposits of the annual
flood of the Nile, or past lives,
but it can fly straight and true across half a planet.
Ibis knows where it is going, and Ibis knows
what it must do when it gets there.
Don't forget that, when it's time for you to transmigrate.

WORM

Immortality   Death

The day is coming – soon we'll meet,
meet in the sweet bye and bye.
And we'll be lovers, you and I.
My dainty flesh will know your bite
And I'll be good enough to eat
you droll hermaphrodite.

DRAGON

Curiosity   World-weariness

If you want to see a dragon
And you haven't seen one yet
Don't you look in a history book
Or on your television set.

You may see one in a rainbow,
In the haloed crescent moon.
They love to dance in the South of France,
But never fear, you'll see one soon.

RAVEN

Sympathy   Xenophobia

Which is crow and which is raven?
Which is brave and which is craven?
Which is raven, which is crow?
Tell the truth now, you don't know.

KOALA

Sensuality   Lasciviousness

Koala has a great big nose,
It's big and black and shiny.
It compensates him for his penis –
Shrivelled up and tiny.

DODO

Inspiration   Plagiarism

Long ago on a tiny island there lived a handsome dodo named Horace. He dreamed of his own posterity, and built himself a monument more enduring than brass. Pirates came and went, plying the blighted ocean in their search for loot, only to find the gallows tree or a watery grave, and none ever disturbed the immortal shrine that Horace had contrived. And to this day the lonesome dodo lingers on, preserved for all time in the uttermost reaches of that surging ocean within the poet's heart, where none can find him and, to all intents and purposes, he is extinct.

TOAD

Tolerance   Apathy

A slimy toad sat by his swamp
Rattling his tambourine
His skin was green and cold and damp
Glistening with brilliantine.
A stranger passing caught his eye
And said "Who's stranger, you or I?"

GOAT

Godliness   Moral Bankruptcy

Despite his pointy goatee beard,
His cloven hoof, his antic horn,
His ruttish smell, his aspect weird,
Everyone loves a Capricorn.

FOX

Grace   Ingratitude

Baby fox is born in Spring,
By Summer he's fully grown.
His marriage is an Autumn thing;
By Winter he's alone.
Once a rascal, now he's wise instead
And once the Spring returns, why, he'll be dead.

SHARK

Courage   Folly

You ancient, you modern, too modern to sleep
You nibble the titbits of time all day long.
The children you nurture, the tears that you weep
Become you like scars on the brave and the strong.

LOBSTER

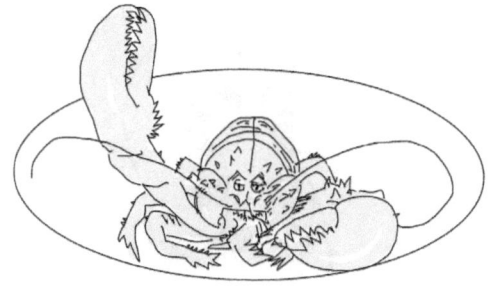

Illusion   Delusion

Slow motion scuttling through ocean bed's litter,
A lobster retires to her temple within
There to forget both the sour and the bitter
That poisons a life on the debris of sin.
Tender sweet flesh in a hideous shell:
Transcendent bliss in a vision from Hell.

ROOSTER

Alarm   Armageddon

O Cruel and Haughty Poultry Birdie.
Pedantic, proud, punctilious scratcher
(Dearie mark my wordie wordie)
Beady eyed like Margaret Thatcher
Chanticleer, fine feathers flaunting,
Pusillaminous, scatological,
Strutting, rutting, farmyard haunting,
Blasphemous and diabolical
In the morning be my clock
Wake me up and call me "cock".

POSSUM

Nuisance   Torment.

Who's that stomping on the roof all night
Wearing out their size ten hobnail boots?
Nipping Mother's roses in the bud?
Peeling lemons hanging on the tree?
Squabbling with the bastard neighbour's cat?
Psychopathic rooting with their mates?

Forget about the local council's traps
You're not allowed to catch them any more.
Go and fetch the plastic snakes and owls
Boil the garlic, camphor, peppermint
And vinegar to daub along the fence
Then call the travel agent, book a flight
New Zealand is the place to buy a coat
Or gloves or scarf of vermin possum fur.
Just be warm and cosy, might as well,
Until they stomp across the roof of Hell.

THYLACINE

Proof   Faith

I have seen
A Thylacine
I hope you will believe me

And why should I
Tell you a lie?
Your doubts would just aggrieve me

It's not as though
A UFO
Has beamed me up and probed me

Or I had seen
On Halloween
A Succubus who disrobed me

I did not meet
On Swanson Street
A Big Foot or a Yeti

I never saw

A Greek Centaur
A Golem or a Fairy

Just what I said
Not off my head
You ought to give me credit

A Thylacine
Is what I seen
I meant it if I said it

THE BLOWFLY IN WINTER

Foresight   Fata Morgana

Erratic, bloated and cumbersome,
Monstrous and out of season,
Summoning up omens and portents,
Comets and cows with two heads,
Black and blurred, noisy, disgusting,
Too gross, it would seem, too fat to fly.

Quick kill the rooster, examine his entrails,
Release the doves, release the pigeons,
Too much salt and not enough water,
Too much bile and not enough justice,
Too much phlegm and not enough sweat,
Too much blood, too much blood.
Throw the big fat book away –
Attend instead to what the blowfly has to say.

ACKNOWLEDGMENTS

Acknowledgments and thanks are due to:

Hooligan Street Poetry who published my poem "Queen" online.

Ron Barassi and the Melbourne FC, whose tragi-comic adventures simulated the backstory of my literary life.

Nick, my brother whose tireless support and encouragement, as well as his fine illustrations, made my dreams coalesce into reality.

Annie, my goddaughter whose enthusiasm and expertise sustains my dreams of showbiz.

Mungo and Roy, my sons whose role as unwitting sounding board helped me to refine and ameliorate my art.

Maxine, my muse.

www.ingramcontent.com/pod-product-compliance
Lightning Source LLC
Chambersburg PA
CBHW060346080526
44583CB00014B/1082